ON RACISM

Essays on Black Popular Culture,
African American Politics,
and the New Black Aesthetics

Earnest N. Bracey

University Press of America,® Inc.
Lanham · Boulder · New York · Toronto · Oxford

Copyright © 2003 by
University Press of America,® Inc.
4501 Forbes Boulevard
Suite 200
Lanham, Maryland 20706
UPA Acquisitions Department (301) 459-3366

PO Box 317
Oxford
OX2 9RU, UK

ISBN 0-7618-2596-7 (paperback : alk. ppr.)

Dedication

To my colleague, friend, and extraordinary mentor—

Dr. Leslie B. McLemore.

Table of Contents

Acknowledgments

I would like to personally thank Robert Fuhrel for his encouraging words after having read the manuscript. I especially appreciate his comments and suggestions on the first draft of this work.

The process of writing the essays in this book has left me emotionally exhausted. However, this book would not have been possible without assistance from my wife. I am deeply grateful for her help.

Introduction

This book examines iconoclastic notions of racial politics, racism, history, and racialism in light of our continuing democratic and cultural development. It investigates our practical understanding of race, popular culture, politics and black aesthetics, and the logic of how we should understand and inquire about the reality of these important things to gain human knowledge. Indeed, one must ask: How do we understand the specific order of these things or notions? Moreover, why should any of these notions be important to our way of thinking? What is so intrinsically significant about these subjects?

In the theoretical sense, of course, racism and racialism are much maligned and misunderstood ideologies, but the widespread interest exemplified in race, racism, and pragmatic Black or Afrocentric thought in America today is significant because it is a reflection of the present day crisis of consciousness, aesthetics, culture, politics, and our truth seeking. According to Alden Vaughan, a professor of history at Columbia University, "Racism is relatively systematic and internally consistent. In time it acquires a pseudo-scientific veneer that glosses over its irrationalities and enables it to claim intellectual respectability" (1995, p. ix).

Vaughan goes on to define racism or racial discrimination as the "unequal treatment of someone on the basis of his or her presumed racial affiliation" (1995, p. ix). Therefore, if Vaughan is correct, we must also try to understand our prejudices and existence as humans, as well as come to grips with our purpose and differences in life. We must also embrace our varied separate and conflicting attitudes, opinions and cultures, as well as the absolute "truth of things." Presumably, it is the very nature of the discussion of these matters that allows us to penetrate more deeply into what is going on in our polarized society today concerning the "calculus" of racism and race relations. And these contentious issues should be of crucial interest to all Americans, or everyone in the world today, for that matter.

Certainly the historical time (or particular historical circumstances) have played an important role in our collective knowledge, but it must be pointed out that such an understanding is essential to conduct a thorough and complete investigation or review of *racism* and *racial* politics in a free-market democracy. Even more importantly, we should be concerned with how the two terms coincide or coalesce with the issues already discussed; and especially how they will be presented in this work.

Toward this end, we must recognize that so-called human groups (or races) are only a means of human identification, codification, or characterization. In recent years, there has been a growing awareness that there are no *real* distinctions between human-kind—in terms of genetics; therefore, it is necessary to emphasize that *racialism* and *racism* are often used interchangeably, but the latter is better used to refer to "prejudice or hostility towards [different] people because of their racial origin, or whether or not this [is] linked to a developed racial theory" (Heywood, 1998, p. 228).

What Heywood points out in the above statement is what many black intellectuals and scholars know and have already emphasized; that is, "racialist thinkers have often denied the existence of a single human species and treated races as if they are separate species" (Heywood, 1998, p. 228). Furthermore, we must understand that racism, as a racial ideology, "has always opposed [the] myth of a person's mind as a private museum where the meaning of the words he understands are exhibited [only] to him" (Murphy, 1990, p. 80). This is to say, racism "demonstrates that things that are made up are also real, that social constructs can have sinister social causes and consequences" (Lipsitz, 1998, p. 176).

In addition, we must inquire: What are the essential characteristics of this particular phenomenon of racism? Or what difference does it make? It is important here to remind oneself that "race is a fiction, that no basis exists in biology or anthropology to categorize people along racial lines" (Lipsitz, 1998, p. 176). This last point is particularly important to note, especially in regards to the relation between *racism* and *racialism*, because as public intellectual Ashley Montagu has written:

> The history of the concept of race is a truly dreadful one. From its beginning and by its very existence, the term has served to narrow the definition of humanity through the establishment of an hegemonic hierarchy of discrete entities. These entities, the so-called races, were primarily based on differences

in physical traits. Such physical traits were soon linked with cultural and social differences, educability, and intelligence. (Montagu, 1997, p. 285)

Attempts, moreover, have been made to define *racism* not only in popular culture or aesthetic terms, but also in a postmodernist context. Yet none of these means or ways offer a full explanation of how we can use racialism in the discussion of race in the post modernist United States. Post modernism, for example, "is a controversial and confusing term.... Post modernists argue that there is no such thing as certainty: the idea of absolute and universal truth must be discarded as an arrogant pretense. Emphasis is instead placed on discourse, debate and democracy" (Heywood, 1998, p. 324). This says that there is something *paradoxical* and even *cathartic* about a discussion of race and racism.

The point here is to recognize the dichotomy and difficulties that currently exist among different racial ideologies and philosophies, and among the various cultures of people in the United States today. Although these are hardly complicated ideologies or theories, race and racism are vast subjects. Nevertheless, we must understand that racism is "a subordinate category within other forms of economic and political domination" (Lipsitz, 1998, pp. 176-177). Thus, racialism and racism, in postmodernist America, as I have already pointed out, are ways of comparing and analyzing, prophetically, the historical and institutional racist record, so that we can widen our perceptions and horizon about what ails us as a people and as a heterogeneous and complex nation.

And racism, no matter how you view it, or deny it, is still the problem of our time. However, the term does not *explicitly* set out to argue—to any degree—for absolute truth. Even more important, an understanding of *racism* does not solve our racial problems, or social exigencies; however, we will try to present a novel way of explaining racism and race in this work. Racism, in general, is a policy view or a pedagogical ideology of independent thought that responds negatively to human nature, as well as to human suffering in terms of ethnicity, human development, cultural differences, aesthetics and distinctive social and political behavior.

Challenging or confronting racists gives one the possibility of dealing with the problems of white supremacy (or racism), and an increasingly hostile and conservative climate in America for African Americans and other minorities. Moreover, it must be clearly understood that race is not a determinant of human behavior. (Montagu, 1997, p. 9) Nor is it regarded as a distinctively American philosophy in that other nations also discriminate.

Further, many of the critical issues and questions in this book do not always, or necessarily have a single answer. This is to say that recognizing racism is not offered here as a way of coping completely with absolute reality. For example, what exactly will invoke reason about the myth of race? Whatever the precise explanation about these contentious issues, *racism* will always mean that because of our differences in belief regarding race, there will be humans who will always, perhaps, believe they are superior to others.

The chapters within this volume fit within a political and social framework so that, considered as a whole, it illustrates how the idea of racism in American popular culture has affected all Americans. One of the main purposes of this book is to persuade the reader that we must examine our various histories and widely held beliefs, as well as our basic and sometimes false assumptions about what is credible, as in the chapter on "The Black Writer's Struggle For Integrity." The historical reflection on W.E.B. Du Bois tells us that many Americans are still in denial about race. But if African Americans don't write their history, someone else will.

Indeed, in order to know ourselves, we must know our history, especially when it comes to understanding the challenges of the black scholar today. Equally important, we must accept that there is no such thing as true racial equality in contemporary America. Therefore, it is impossible to form an accurate picture of the world (and the United States) in which we live without acknowledging these problems and 'hard truths' such as with the revival of scientific racism. The chapter on scientific racism and how former black slaves fought supposedly for the Confederacy is another story altogether. But it is a story that must be told. Although we can simply look directly at our historical situations, these political issues delve much deeper into our cultural psyche. But, befitting the highly political elements of the racial issue, some scholars believe that we can examine even the depths of our tortured souls, dissect the despair, and define what ails us as a nation. Alas, we must know that this is the complicated world in which we operate.

Furthermore, the thoughts and analysis presented here about Francis Fukuyama's *The End of History and the Last Man* let us know that it should not be difficult to overstate the enormity of the racial situation in the United States. In other words, the questions of race and multiculturalism are still major challenges in our society today. Therefore, we must address these hard topics or issues with honesty and with some conviction.

As far as the chapter on black leaders is concerned, we must invoke, as some black scholars do, the axiom, "Thou shall not write or speak ill of a fellow black person"—that is, if it is conceivably possible. In other words,

African Americans should not take each other for granted intellectually or otherwise, no matter the circumstances. This simple message should speak volumes about the desire of African Americans to find a new voice and apt leader for the psychologically drained and embattled Black Community.

At issue is an emotional debate over who should lead in the black community during the next millennium. Which is to say, there is consternation about the very point about who should actually lead. However, since black leaders do not speak in one voice, black people's leverage in this country's political system is not proportional to the political power and demands they can or might achieve. Black politicians, however, invariably fall into the inevitable category of leadership, no matter who they speak for or represent.

The fact that racism is even pervasive in Africa among blacks, as journalist Keith B. Richburg points out in his book, *Out of America*, has certainly made it hard to stop or contain. Indeed, what have been the consequences of "black racism" (or black bigotry, for that matter), and the efforts to establish a multi-racial world? The harsh truth is that, sadly enough, many Americans don't want to solve the *intractable* problem of race. In fact, many people in the United States today don't even see race or racism as a major problem or concern.

In the case of the chapter on black aesthetics and popular culture and the analysis of the sexually explicit novels—*The Life and Loves of Mr. Jiveass Nigger and How to Make Love to a Negro*—one must be cognizant that blacks in America have always had to deal with their mythical or so-called super-human sexuality. They have also had to fight, especially during the modern-day civil rights movement, to challenge, to protest, to resist the dominant culture that has always controlled American laws and racist-inspired policies. An interesting corollary of this point, as both of these popular and racy novels indicate, is that many blacks see their existence in the court systems throughout the Unites States as a way of limiting every aspect of their lives. As a general matter, black males are unproportionately on death row and physically warehoused in our prisons. Thus, we must clearly understand that the struggle in our courts for African Americans ranges across the landscape of our national and personal lives. Ultimately, black males are sometimes unfairly and unduly affected by our judicial system and seen as villains. From this point of view, there have been grave miscarriages of justice in our court system.

In the chapter on Dr. Seuss's the *Sneetches*, one must seek reconciliation and work together as a people (the human race), to show tolerance of others who are different; that is, in order to build the kind of righteous community necessary to survive as a multi-racial democracy. And with regards to the existence of race and similar classifications or stratifications, as addressed by the late Dr. Seuss, Professor Randall Kennedy of Harvard University had this to say:

> The fact that race matters…does not mean that the salience and consequences of racial distinctions are good or that race must continue to matter in the future. Nor does the brute sociological fact that race matters dictate what one's response to that fact should be. (1997, p. 64)

It is worth noting that many African Americans are not necessarily optimistic about our nation or their future. Black Americans, however, must *never* give up, or allow a kind of 'conspiracy of silence' to take over—that is, they must never stop short of the crucial dialogue that is so vital for us to exist as a society. Here is a nightmare scenario: We stop communicating and start fighting each other again—as in our past Civil War—in a bloody race war, as envisioned in the last chapter about an imaginary Race War in the United States in the year 2010.

Finally, if one is to get anything out of this volume, one must try to conscientiously seek to raise more pertinent questions about *racism* and the racial problem of our nation. We must also reveal the truth about ourselves. And most importantly, we must learn more about our country's rich and complex racial history.

We must also try to find answers and solutions to the things we have been grappling with since the inception of our fragile nation, such as the new political culture of mean-spiritedness, racism, intolerance—the social sickness of segregation, discrimination, bigotry, white supremacy, prejudice, collective ignorance, and our own psyche wounds or individual fears. In the final analysis, we must put forward in our national psyche or consciousness, if possible, a way to eliminate race and racism, which will call for the reinvigoration of a sane, sober, sophisticated intellectual and philosophical life in America. It will also require a regeneration of social forces, empowering the disadvantaged, degraded, and dejected. We must finally reject "the faddish cynicism and fashionable conservatism rampant in the intelligentsia and general populace." (West, 1989, p. 239)

REFERENCES

Heywood, Andrew. 1998. *Political Ideologies: An Introduction*. New York: Worth Publishers.

Kennedy, Randall. May, 1997. "My Race Problem—and Ours." *The Atlantic Monthly*.

Lipsitz, George. 1998. *The Possessive Investment in Whiteness: How White People Profit From Identity Politics*. Philadelphia: Temple University Press.

Montagu, Ashley. 1997. *Man's Most Dangerous Myth: The Fallacy of Race*. 6th edition. Walnut Creek, California: Alta Press.

Murphy, John P. 1990. *Pragmatism: From Pierce to Dardson*. Boulder, Colorado: Westview Press.

Vaughan, Alden T. 1995. *Roots of American Racism: Essays on the Colonial Experience*. New York: Oxford University Press.

West, Cornel. 1989. *The American Evasion of Philosophy: A Genealogy of Pragmatism*. Madison, Wisconsin: The University of Wisconsin Press.

The Black Writer's Struggle for Integrity

ON THE ART OF BLACK WRITING

From the start, it must be clearly understood that the study of literature and human behavior may be both interesting and practical: it is also important to know that "the relationship between fact and [literary] theory in...[writing] is not nearly so straight forward" as the general public (or popular authors) has led us to believe. "The layman usually thinks of a theory [and writing] as an attempt to make sense out of a mass of accumulated fact, but [another] function of [theoretical writing] is to define a problem in objective terms that will permit relevant facts to be gathered" (Jonas, 1973, p. 57). Therefore, writing an exact account of a black person's life, based on facts and theories, is perhaps the best way to explain human development and black writing. The late and eminent psychologist Abraham H. Maslow would perhaps agree with this method of understanding human experiences—that is, the art of writing stories or biographies from an African American's point of view or perspective—as he wrote:

> Esthetic experience, creative experience, love experience, mystic experience, insight experience, and other peak-experiences are pre-consciously taken for granted and commonly expected by artists and art educators, by creative teachers, by religious and philosophical theorists, by loving husbands, mothers and therapists and by many others. (Maslow, 1968, p. 102)

But one might wonder what value there can be in understanding theories about a black person's life-time of behavior and development? Indeed, can a particular book, or biographical profile, or even short stories about 'black-life' be of interest to *anyone* but black people, or those black nationalist scholars and laymen interested in studying African American aesthetics, psychology, personalities, and human behavior?

An obvious answer is: Yes, of course. In any theory about writing, according to Nobel Prize winning novelist Toni Morrison, "the crucial distinction…is not the difference between fact and fiction, but the distinction between fact and truth" (1995, p. 93). Toward this end, and even more significant, *fiction* can also serve as the truth, or vice-versa. Generally though, an intuitive and analytical approach to writing is also important.

One must understand, moreover, that a person's biographical testimony or oral history can sometimes be biased or *unreliable*, maybe even unrealistic. Nevertheless, as Louis Alexander tells us, "with the facts in [a] story on which the emotional responses are based, the reader can judge the validity of the emotions raised by the [particular] story" (Alexander, 1975, p. 20). This contention might be true of any writing.

Another probable bias in understanding a person's life is the fact that sometimes the information might be obtained by devious, dishonest, or perhaps shady means. Further, there is sometimes contradiction in what one writes. In fact, one must be cognizant that some authors, especially biographers, will sometimes:

> do almost anything to get information: lie; steal; betray confidences; make false promises; quote "off the record" remarks; expose their confidential sources; use anonymous and questionable witnesses, some of whom will say anything for spite or money, ferret through garbage; masquerade as doctors, policemen, friends, relatives; threaten, intimidate, blackmail, or trick people into spilling the beans. (Brian, 1994, p. 37)

Such unorthodox and unethical methods of obtaining information must also be taken into account when the black writer considers *any* materials upon which his work is based, because it, too, (or the material) may be rendered unreliable, or even *contrived* to support an author's prejudicial or biased beliefs. As professors Jacques Barzun and Henry F. Graff have written: "In assessing bias, the [writer] must bring to bear a certain sophistication of mind. As a thoughtful scholar he recognizes the double condition of the search for truth— it must in the end produce a form and at any point it answers some implied or expressed interest" (Barzun & Graff, 1992, p. 187).

Expressed interest, finally, can be *stymied* if the information supposedly available is not accessible to the writer or biographer. As historian Morris J. MacGregor succinctly explains:

The problem for the modern researcher [or writer] is that...special collections [especially concerning racial subjects] and reserved materials, no longer classified and no longer sensitive, have fallen, largely unnoted, into a sea of...paper beyond the reach of the archivist's finding aids. [Therefore], the frequently expressed comment of the [biographer is], "somebody is withholding something..." [or] "somebody has lost track of something" (MacGregor, 1981, p. 625).

MacGregor also correctly states that: "subterfuges [are] employed from time to time by [writers] dealing with racial subjects" (MacGregor, 1981, p. 625). In other words, records and documents that might shed light on a subject or tell the whole story about a historical life are sometimes deliberately destroyed or misplaced, perhaps, because of some biases, or prejudice.

Moreover, in any black biography or life history, one must clearly understand that, "improperly written and arranged, such stories [or personal histories] amount to biased reporting or to propaganda. The difference lies in presentation of evidence in the story itself, including contradictory statements and even evidence that may not support the writer's own view of what the situation means and what the facts add up to" (Alexander, 1975, p. 20).

In the ultimate analysis, it is *extremely* important that a personal narrative of events, or written account of one's life—that is, a life history—must be accurate to the point that it is free, as much as possible, from bias.

ON BEING AND WRITING

When the famous black writer and best-selling author from Mississippi, Richard Wright, wrote his first book of autobiographical short stories, *Uncle Tom's Children*, it was hailed by the late and great novelist, Ralph Ellison, as an expression of "artistic sensibility overcoming the social and cultural isolation of Negro [black] life and moving into a world of unlimited intellectual and imaginative possibilities" (Wright, 1940 and 1965; Ellison, 1987, pp. 198-216). Hence, writing about one's personal growth and development with honesty and integrity and without apology takes great moral courage and conviction. In fact, *Uncle Tom's Children* is the epitome of such important and courageous writing.

It has been over fifty years since Wright's first published book, and despite the many changes in the modern-day South, especially after the enactment of the Civil Rights Act of 1964, the lot of many impoverished blacks has not drastically improved. Indeed, growing up in Mississippi, I have found that the more things in Mississippi (and elsewhere) have changed for black Americans—socially, economically and/or otherwise—the more they have remained the same. This is to say, many poor blacks are still at the bottom of the totem pole, so to speak, in Mississippi and elsewhere in our society.

The deplorable situation that exists for some blacks, of course, is a sad commentary on equal opportunity and race relations in this country. None-theless, blacks in America have survived in a 'displaced world' because they ultimately have refused to roll over and play dead when confronted with controversy, unspeakable acts of cruelty, and terrible hardships.

Richard Wright explored some of these intractable racial themes in *Uncle Tom's Children*, and his brilliant collections of short stories continue to be praised as a work of raw, literary talent and courage. As a fellow Mississippian, I, too, have tried to understand what motivated Richard Wright to write such per-sonal and compassionate stories. The late James Baldwin, one of America's foremost black writers, in his classic book of essays, *Notes of a Native Son*, wrote:

> As for [the] New Negro, it was Wright who became his most eloquent spokesman; and his work, from its beginning, is most clearly committed to the social struggle. Leaving aside the considerable question of what relationship precisely the artist bears to the [black] revolutionary, the reality of man as a social being is not his only reality and that artist is strangled who is forced to deal with human beings solely in social terms; and who has, moreover, as Wright had, the necessity thrust on him of being the representative of [black] people. (Baldwin, 1955 and 1983, pp. 32-33)

Richard Wright's multilayered and engaging prose, however, accurately portrays the trials, sufferings, and tribulations of blacks in the South. In his other works, such as *Native Son*, he also tried to explain how black people have tried to escape poverty, indignity, and their miserable existence by mi-grating to other parts of the country for a better life.

It must be understood that those who have previously investigated the subject of race have dealt chiefly with those experiences that always plague black Americans. And in this perspective, many black writers of note devote "much of their work to exploring what the literary theorist Houston Baker calls 'the African-American Autobiographical moment'—in a genre dubbed 'autocritography' by [Henry L.] Gates" of Harvard University who believes that a black person's "experiences, however personal, are automatically his-torical" (Boynton, 1995, p. 62).

In many critical ways, the theories and philosophies of Zen Buddhism and *existentialism*, as with all of our lives, also affirm the freedom and responsibility of the individual. Thus, one can earnestly incorporate Sartre's discussion of *Being*. And like Richard Wright, whose "philosophical interest[s] stemmed from his early existential experiences as well as from the sense of being both inside and outside American culture" (Wright & Fabre, 1997, p. xiii), one must try (absolutely) to show how the broader sense of blacks' *Being* and survival in the Diaspora remains a serious, contentious and important issue. Indeed, how does one rightly view life, in general, for blacks in the United States? It is even evident in Sartre's philosophical writings that he understood instinctively the existence or meaning of *Being* and *Life* for all humans, but especially African Americans. Sartre wrote:

> Being is. Being is in-itself. Being is what it is. Being includes both Being-in-itself and Being-for-itself, but the latter is the nihilation of the former. As contrasted with Existence, Being is all-embracing and objective rather than individual and subjective. (1956, p. 629)

Why is this passage by Sartre so important for black writers? It is significant because over a lifetime, our attitudes, beliefs and different preoccupations change. Consequently, as psychoanalyst Eric Berne pointed out, "In a given individual, a certain set of behavior patters corresponds to one's state of mind, while another set is related to a different psychic attitude, often inconsistent with the first" (Berne, 1964, p. 23). In addition, the late existential analyst and philosopher Rollo May has written that, "by discovering and affirming the *being* in ourselves...inner certainty will become possible" (1983, p. 10). May goes on clearly to write that:

> We all seem in our culture to be hesitant to talk of Being. Is it too revealing, too intimate, too profound? In covering up Being we lose just those things we most cherish in life. For the sense of Being is bound up with the questions that are deepest and most fundamental—questions of love, death, anxiety, [and] caring. (1983, p. 10)

Therefore, and in the strictest sense, one must try to write about the *Being* and all of the tragic and gut-wrenching things that go along with life and living—and without sugar-coating these things to appeal to the taste of certain individuals, or a wider-public. However, the public at large can perhaps learn from the particular circumstances of some of these "birth-to-adult" or "cradle-to-grave" events presented in all such autobiographies and biographies. One must also have a fascination of the black aesthetic that will perhaps drive the writing.

Essentially, as MacArthur Genius Award Winner and American Book
Award recipient Charles Johnson has written some things, such as, "natural-
ism seemed to conceal profound prejudices about Being, what a person is,
the nature of society, causation, and…metaphysical questions about what could
and could not logically occur in our "experience" and conscious life" (Johnson,
1990, p. 6). In essence, black writing must be about seeking philosophical
truths in a racist world that hasn't really changed very much, since the inception of the country, especially by today's standards.

In this sense, Johnson's astute reflections and analyses are almost Zen-like
in tone, prompting us to address seriously rhetorical questions such as the
following.

> Where are we going…? If nowhere, why this effort, why walk on? The answer
> is that we still walk on, on a path that is trodden within, yet on steps which lie
> without—yet where the treading is neither in nor out but just a constant
> treading, just a joyful yet compassionate, relaxed yet strenuous moving with
> the flow of life to its own inseverable identity of every part in a living and
> unending whole. (Humphreys, 1992, p. 164)

CONCLUSIONS

In many profound instances, the answers to our human development (and
behavior) exist across our entire life-cycle, or spectrum of life. Hence, autobiographical stories must try not only to gain an understanding of the major
literary theories and ideas to explain the 'coming of age' of young black men
and women in a traditionally racist society, but also such thoughts and theories
should attempt to reveal the soul and character of those who have the courage to challenge the status-quo and, of course, a discriminatory system.
Furthermore, literary patterns or theories, as well as complex and philosophical themes, should support and enhance a person's fictional account or writing.
Indeed, these important things, or underlying reasons, are necessary to make
real connections and gain a deeper and pragmatic insight into the forces that
influence a black person's life. In the final analysis, all black writing must be
taken seriously, and as Robert I. Berkman reminds us in his book, *Find It Fast*,
"authors [must] typically have a solid and in-depth understanding of their
subject. They [must also] possess a broad view of their field and…provide
excellent background information" (Berkman, 1987, p. 164). All in all, one
must also consider that:

> If becoming an adult is a task that requires power and expertise, it's easy to see
> why it is so difficult. When we are born, we have very little of either. All of the

power and the expertise is in other people, and we are so very much smaller than they are.... As we continue to grow, however, and increase in wisdom and stature, we gain more ability and expertise to do things through the processes of internalization and identification. (Cloud, 1992, p. 284)

Finally, in order to be effective in obtaining the information and knowledge necessary to understand a black person's life, the researcher or writer must ultimately "do some background reading in the subject area...[which consists] of looking up [the] subject or topic in general reference works—encyclopedias, biographical dictionaries, or books...." (Weidenborner & Carious, 1994, p. 9) In this way, the writer becomes an effective recorder of historical events.

Furthermore, in writing personal stories about black Americans, we must use the ideas and theories made available to us by poets, writers, philosophers, and scholars who believe anyone's life ultimately is worth learning about and recording. Moreover, as humans, we must continue to grow and develop writing skills—to advance ourselves to even higher and loftier writing and intellectual goals and standards. And in doing so, black writing will change for the better. In conclusion, and as Maslow once emphatically pointed out:

When the philosophy of man (his nature, his goals, his potentialities, his fulfillment) changes, then everything changes, not only the philosophy of politics, of economics, of ethics and values, of interpersonal relations and of history itself, but also the philosophy of education, of psychotherapy and of personal growth, the theory of how to help men become what they can and deeply need to become. (1968, p. 189)

REFERENCES

Alexander, Louis. 1975. *Beyond The Facts: A Guide to the Art of Feature Writing.* Houston, Texas: Gulf Publishing Company.

Baldwin, James. 1955 and 1983. *Notes of a Native Son.* Boston, Massachusetts: Beacon Press.

Barzun, Jacques & Graff, Henry F. 1992. *The Modern Researcher.* 5th edition. Orlando, Florida: Harcourt Brace Jovanovich.

Berkman, Robert I. 1987. *Find It Fast: How to Uncover Expert Information on Any Subject.* New York: Harper & Row.

Berne, Eric. 1964. *Games People Play: The Psychology of Human Relationships.* New York: Grove Press, Inc.

Boynton, Robert S. 1995, March. "The New Intellectuals." *The Atlantic Monthly*.

Brian, Denis. 1994. *Fair Game: What Biographers Don't Tell You*. Amherst, New York: Prometheus Books.

Cloud, Henry. 1992. *Changes that Heal: How to Understand Your Past to Ensure a Healthier Future*. New York: Harper Paperbacks.

Ellison, Ralph. 1987. *Going To The Territory*. New York: Vintage Books.

Humphreys, Christmas. 1992. *Zen: A Way Of Life*. Chicago, Illinois: NTC Publishing Group.

Johnson, Charles. 1990. *Being and Race: Black Writing Since 1970*. Indianapolis: Indiana University Press.

Jonas, Gerald. 1973. *Visceral Learning: Toward A Science Of Self-Control*. New York: The Viking Press.

MacGregor, Morris J. Jr. 1981. *Integration of the Armed Forces 1940–1965*. Washington, D.C.: Center of Military History, United States Army.

Maslow, Abraham H. 1968. *Toward a Psychology of Being*. New York: Van Nostrand Reinhold Company.

May, Rollo. 1983. *The Discovery of Being: Writings in Existential Psychology*. New York: W. W. Norton and Company.

Morrison, Toni. 1995. "The Site of Memory." *Inventing the Truth: The Art and Craft of Memoir*. William Zinsser, editor. 2nd edition. New York: Houghton Mifflin Company.

Sartre, Jean-Paul. 1956. *Being and Nothingness: The Major Text of Existentialism*. Translated by Hazel E. Barnes. New York: Gramercy Books.

Weidenborner, Stephen & Caruso, Domenick. 1994. *Writing Research Papers: A Guide to the Process*. 4th edition. New York: St. Martin's Press.

Wright, Ellen & Fabre, Michel. editors. 1997. *Richard Wright Reader*. New York: DaCapo Press.

Wright, Richard. 1940 and 1965. *Uncle Tom's Children*. Back flap. New York: Harper and Row Publishers.

Remembering a Black Scholar: The Ideological and Intellectual Life of William Edward Burghardt Du Bois (1868–1963)

W.E.B. Du Bois is recognized as the preeminent black scholar of his day. He was especially brilliant when it came to articulating black aesthetics and black protest in America. Du Bois was born in Great Barrington, Massachusetts, in 1868 from intelligent, concerned, and educated parents, Alfred and Mary, who encouraged his scholarly pursuits.

During the time of his life, many considered him to be egotistical, introverted, or even arrogant, because of his famous aloofness. But he was never mean-spirited. In some quarters, moreover, Du Bois was thought of as a "wunderkind," a genius of sorts because he already had a B.A. from predominantly black Fisk University before being accepted to Harvard as an undergraduate and later graduate student.

Attending Harvard had always been a dream of his, and Du Bois was extremely flattered and delighted when he was accepted, as he was confident in his academic abilities to compete successfully with whites. In the end, Du Bois was the first African American to graduate from prestigious Harvard University, receiving his Ph.D. in 1895.

W.E.B. Du Bois must also be given credit for his intellectual prowess, which was a reflection of his capabilities, and he excelled as a student and a black scholar, going on to study and train as a social scientist at Berlin University in Germany. Du Bois, however, was never a braggart or one to pat himself on the back because he felt it was his duty and obligation to tell the truth about America in a sensible and intelligent way.

Indeed, all he really wanted to do was to keep the dialogue going about 'race relations,' and to explain where Americans—both black and white—were headed as a nation. More importantly, Du Bois wanted to show that blacks were the equal to whites and to explain ways in which African Americans could achieve economic and educational parity. This, of course, was the major reason he wanted to study the Negro, or blacks in depth in America.

Why did studying African Americans even matter to Du Bois? In a nutshell, it was important to him because of the prevalence of *racism* and discrimination in America. As a highly educated and sophisticated black academic, for example, Du Bois couldn't even find a permanent position at a White Institution, not even at his alma-mater, Harvard.

And even when Du Bois was hired *temporarily* at predominantly black Wilberforce in Philadelphia, after his graduate studies, he was given the dubious 'assistant instructorship' title for $900 annually. But for a year, the money paid his bills and allowed him to marry his first wife, Nina.

Perhaps, in retrospect, his non-selection to white institutions as a professor led him to teach at predominantly black universities or black institutions of higher education in the South, where he thrived intellectually. Specifically, he taught economics, sociology, and history at Atlanta University, starting in 1897.

When Du Bois first started out as an academic and university professor, with his enhanced education and knowledge, all he wanted to do was study the great works and write thoughtful and important books about black people. In that way, he thought he could make a real difference in the world. Indeed, those times were some of his most fruitful and productive years, as he was at first able to study and reflect and not go outside of a comfortable box he had psychologically created for himself.

But Du Bois was deeply disturbed, 'shakened to the core' of his being, or shocked to his very fiber, when he learned of the brutal lynching of a black man named Sam Hose in April of 1897. Hose was burned after his death by a white mob of several thousand people. To add insult to injury, many of these whites of Atlanta, Georgia even took parts of his charred and mutilated body as souvenirs; and this left a chilling and indelible impression on Du Bois' mind.

Supposedly, Sam Hose had killed a white farmer during a bitter argument, but Du Bois noted, sadly, that Hose was never given a fair trial in a

Court of Law. In fact, Du Bois felt it was a mockery of American justice. All in all, this incident, more than any other, woke Du Bois up from his complacency. Indeed, Du Bois believed he had to do something!

Hence, on July 10, 1905, Du Bois took part in what would be called The Niagara Movement, which took place at Erie Beach Hotel in Ontario, Canada, because of the racism that existed in the United States. The whole purpose of the Niagara Movement was to organize, to gather together 29 black delegates—Young Turks—or northern-educated black men of many professions—to fight against segregation and for the franchisement and equal rights of blacks 'head-on.'

The main problem the Niagara group sought to answer or solve was how to assault the bastions of prejudice and discrimination against blacks, given the persistent and overtness of the American race system, as well as the futility of the 'separate-but-equal' doctrine.

Even more important, and because of his status as an honorable black leader, the formidable Mr. Booker T. Washington (from the famous Tuskegee Institute) was also invited to participate at the Niagara conference, but he stubbornly refused to attend on political grounds, or ideological differences. In fact, Mr. Washington did all he could to perhaps undermine and destroy the momentum of the Niagara Movement, as he played-off the influence he had with the Black Press, portraying the members as being militant and subversive. In the end, the Niagara Movement failed because of a lack of black supports and the group's inability to immediately solve the so-called 'Negro Problem.' Toward this end, Du Bois would often come to say, "How does it feel to be a problem?"

Suffice it to say, W.E.B. Du Bois became a part of the National Association for the Advancement of Colored People (NAACP), becoming one of the founding members of the fledgling NAACP in 1909. It must also be pointed out that in the interracial organization's first incarnation, whites fully funded and dominated the leadership of the NAACP. However, as the Director of Publicity and Research, Du Bois became essentially the chief spokesman, not only for the NAACP, but the black community as well also, because he gave promising black artists and authors a voice and the means of expressing themselves through their writings in the *Crisis Magazine*.

As the official journal of the NAACP, the *Crisis Magazine* became Du Bois' platform—a long-held dream—to reach thousands of blacks (and whites) about the problems of the black man. Moreover, Du Bois proved the *possibility* of a black magazine; that is, it could be successful and eventually pay for itself. By 1910, *Crisis Magazine* had a circulation of 100,000—a considerable number at that time—becoming self-supportive and profitable.

As the editor of *Crisis Magazine*, Du Bois was determined to be independent of the key board members. Unfortunately, some NAACP board members did not see eye-to-eye with Du Bois. Indeed, many of them thought that Du Bois should subordinate himself to the NAACP Board chairman. But Du Bois believed that his integrity as the editor of *Crisis Magazine* would be compromised if he gave in to the leadership of the NAACP. In other words, the NAACP Board members at the time did not uphold his right of free expression and his autonomy as the editor of *Crisis Magazine*, and he would not capitulate.

Du Bois refused for years to give up his sovereignty or control of the acclaimed 'black periodical' but eventually resigned in protest from the NAACP and *Crisis Magazine* after twenty-four years, giving up the coveted editorship, which was the most important black journal of its day. After his resignation, the NAACP still had his indirect support, but Du Bois returned to teach full-time at Atlanta University, where he continued to write brilliantly and publish widely across the academic disciplines.

During this period of time also, Du Bois' book, *The Souls of Black Folk*, was selling extremely well. When Du Bois wrote this important gem of a book in 1903, he had *no* idea how popular it would become. To say the least, he poured his heart out in that particular work, but it was not preachy. Yet, Du Bois was inspired when he wrote it. He was especially proud of his prophetic phrase: "The problem of the twentieth century is the problem of the color line."

This was the period also when Du Bois was, in earnest, brought to the public and political limelight by challenging the beloved black leader, Booker T. Washington. And for some white Americans, Du Bois became a threat to their way of life. Mr. Washington believed in accommodation to white supremacists, or a gradual approach to achieving equality and other rights for blacks, as he *never* publicly protested the lynching, brutality, disfranchisement, and segregation laws in America.

Accommodating to white Americans is where Du Bois drew the line with Mr. Washington. He was especially taken aback, appalled, and disappointed with his famous Atlanta Compromise Speech, where Mr. Washington advocated menial work and industrial education for blacks, as opposed to book learning and intellectual pursuits. To add insult to injury, Du Bois believed Mr. Washington had the unmitigated gall or temerity (through his accommodationist approach) to advise blacks not to challenge their miserable existence and pitiful conditions in life.

But in a profound way, Du Bois understood Washington's predicament, given that he wanted the 'good will' of white benefactors to support his precious Tuskegee Institute and other worthwhile projects and causes for blacks, particularly in the South. In essence, Mr. Washington needed the money from wealthy whites.

Du Bois also turned down Mr. Washington's invitation to become part of his thriving Tuskegee Institute as a learned professor on the school's faculty, with a substantial salary, as Du Bois could never work out the details with Washington. Du Bois also learned that Mr. Washington wanted to recruit him as one of his trusted Lieutenants at Tuskegee. Perhaps, Washington was soured to that idea, too, as the position never materialized, because of Du Bois' staunch independence.

Mr. Washington would later think of Du Bois as an unreserved radical. And perhaps one could say that Washington was right on that score because Du Bois was radical in the sense that he would fight verbally—and in writing—for 'uplifting' the black community, that is, of course, by appropriate and legal means. In fact, Du Bois stressed the idea of a college-educated "Talented Tenth" of young African Americans who could become the future leadership for the black masses.

Mr. Washington and his 'Tuskegee Machine' had enormous power and influence within the black community, as Mr. Washington became the first black man to reach such a high plateau. Du Bois believed you had to respect that. After all, Mr. Washington was extremely popular with White Americans at the time, and he became the designated 'voice' for many blacks, especially in the South. But Mr. Washington would not go unchallenged.

Du Bois was still personally disillusioned with Mr. Washington's social platform—particularly his educational policies and his unabashed 'humbling' of himself to accept what whites were willing to give him.

Some would say that by 1916, and upon the death of Mr. Washington, Du Bois was unexpectedly thrown into the role of black leader for black intellectuals and the black community, perhaps to the chagrin of the white community. Later, Du Bois would come to believe that the pattern of life on earth for blacks was fixed, unchanging —with whites always in a dominant position and blacks in cursed subordinate roles. This realization, of course, enraged Du Bois, mobilizing him to action, and made him advocate black capitalism and 'economic self-sufficiency' for all African Americans.

Later, Du Bois became interested in the ideas and principles of Marxism and Communism. He thought that the economic philosophy of Karl Marx should not be ignored. Indeed, Du Bois also emphasized the importance of studying Marxism, a topic that was rarely brought up in the lexicon of black studies. Du Bois was concerned that black people always stood on the brink of annihilation in the United States, but because of their strong will, African

Americans were able to rebound. Du Bois questioned, however, if Blacks would survive as a race of people. He even wondered if he would ever change his mind about white America.

In the end, Du Bois believed that black people would be responsible for their own salvation and destination. Accordingly, Du Bois felt blacks should create their own cultural identity, and establish, if possible, a common ideology.

When Du Bois retired, finally, from Atlanta University in the late 1940s, he thought his political activist days would be over. Some even believed that Du Bois had divorced himself from the modern-day civil rights movement. However, he was pulled back into the racial equality fray.

Equally important, Du Bois traveled the country during those trying times. It was also during these times that Du Bois believed that America would never change its prejudicial attitudes toward black Americans. Hence, he became part of the nationalist Pan-African Movement, as well as participating in other radical political activities in the United States and elsewhere involving blacks in the Diaspora. Indeed, Du Bois "undertook star-crossed efforts to defeat racism with Pan-Africanism and replace colonialism with communism" (Sleeper, 1997, p. 162). Although Du Bois "is generally accorded by black scholars and political leaders alike the title "Father of Pan-Africanism," there were those social critics who believed Du Bois' "Pan-Africanism was simply a type of "romantic racism" that "got nowhere" (Marable, 1999, p. 75).

Du Bois was considered a radical, a subversive and a danger to the United States government. Du Bois, however, was not shocked by the knowledge, because of his communist involvement. McCarthyism, of course, was at its zenith in the 1950s. Du Bois, however, could not understand why he was thought of as a 'traitor,' a so-called dangerous criminal and an agent of the Soviet Union by the U.S. government. Unfortunately, Du Bois was eventually arrested, finger-printed, and marched-off to federal prison in Washington for his political activities and participation in protesting against the atomic bomb and for peace. In the final analysis, moreover, it was found that the federal government did not have any proof that Du Bois betrayed America.

These were extremely bitter and unpleasant days for Du Bois, especially since he refused to sign any government documents saying that he was not a member of the Communist Party. Later, Du Bois would willingly admit that he was, in fact, a Communist Party member. It should be pointed out that perhaps the only bright spot in his life during these perilous times was his marriage to his second wife, Shirley.

Du Bois was further insulted by not being allowed, initially, to travel to Ghana by the U.S. government, where his friend and black African scholar, Kwame Nkrumah, was that country's president in the early part of the 1950s. However, in the 1960s, Du Bois was given his passport and allowed to visit Africa and Europe. Du Bois also traveled widely in the United States to address national and international black groups. But unlike in America, Du Bois was honored everywhere that he visited. Upon finally settling down in Ghana, with Shirley, battleworn and scarred by the racial battle in America, he truly fell in love with the place. In the final analysis, "W.E.B. Du Bois dedicated himself for nearly a century to the struggle to end racial discrimination, the exploitation of nonwhite people across the globe, and other manifestations of social and political oppression" (Marable, 1999, p. 58). Professor Manning Marable explained it this way:

> Du Bois was arrested for "subversive" activities in 1951, his passport was revoked for years, and his books were widely removed from libraries. Harassed by the FBI and vilified in the press, Du Bois remained proudly defiant. On December 1, 1961, he formally joined the U.S. Communist Party. Several days later, he departed from the United States, relocating to Ghana at the invitation of that nation's president, Kwame Nkrumah. During his last years, Du Bois worked on a lifelong interest, developing an encyclopedia of the black world. (1999, p. viii)

Perhaps Du Bois knew it then, that is, he would stay in Accra, Ghana, until his death in 1963. This is to say, Du Bois would never again live in the United States. Du Bois was an American, but he perhaps felt he was also of Africa. Ultimately, he made it possible to challenge the narrow framework in which white Americans saw and perceived blacks. (That is, black Americans were ignorant and incapable of deep thought and critical thinking.) And this attitude allowed him to confront racism on his own terms. Black intellectuals owe him a tremendous debt of gratitude for paving the ways for all black scholars for their success today. In the end, he died far from America in Accra, Ghana, with his boldest and greatest work (on African Americans) unknown and unpublished to most of the world.

RECOMMENDED READING LIST

Bracey, Earnest N. 1999. *Prophetic Insight: The Higher Education and Pedagogy of African Americans*. Maryland: University Press of America.

DeMarco, Joseph P. 1983. *The Social Thought of W.E.B. Du Bois*. Lanham, Maryland: University Press of America.

Franklin, John H & Meier, August, editors. 1982. *Black Leaders of the Twentieth Century*. Chicago: University of Illinois Press.

Rampersad, Arnold. 1976. *The Art and Imagination of W.E.B. Du Bois*. Cambridge, MA: Harvard University Press.

Reed, Adolph L., Jr. 1997. *W.E.B. Du Bois and American Political Thought: Fabianism and the Color Line*. New York: Oxford University Press.

Sterne, Emma G. 1971. *His Was The Voice: The Life of W.E.B. Du Bois*. New York: Crowell-Collier Press.

Steward, Jeffrey C. 1996. *1001 Things Everyone Should Know About African American History*. New York: Doubleday.

REFERENCES

Marable, Manning. 1999. *Black Leadership: Four Great American Leaders and the Struggle for Civil Rights*. New York: Penguin Books.

Marable, Manning. 1999. First published, 1920. "Introduction." *W.E.B. Du Bois Darkwater: Voices From Within the Veil*. Mineola, New York: Dover Publications, Inc.

Sleeper, Jim. 1997. *Liberal Racism*. New York: Viking.

The New Challenge of a Black Scholar

THE BLACK SCHOLAR AS INTELLECTUAL

As a young, neophyte undergraduate, my intellectual appetite was whetted not only by good books and the proverbial classics, but also by the first-rate black scholars and intellectuals that I had the privilege of learning from and being acquainted with for four productive years at a small, predominantly black university in Mississippi. That wonderful school setting provided me with the intellectual freedom and academic or educational wherewithal to compete successfully later with students who graduated from more prestigious and elite white colleges and universities.

Appropriately enough, that educational foundation also allowed me to compete in my professional life, particularly when I decided to undertake my graduate studies and take a terminal Ph.D. degree. To say the least, I was well prepared, despite the sometimes frustrating educational obstacles and circumstances I had to endure in getting a higher education. That is to say, unfortunately I was never perceived as an intellectual equal by many of the white professors with whom I came in contain. Harvard Professor Cornel West aptly voiced a similar concern and dilemma—that is, as a graduate student, when he wrote:

> It is much more difficult for black students, especially graduate students, to be taken seriously as *potential scholars and intellectuals* owing to the managerial ethos of our universities and colleges (in which less time is spent with students) and to the vulgar (racist) perceptions fueled by affirmative action programs which pollute many black student-white professor relations. (1993, p. 69)

Moreover, it must be made abundantly clear that the black scholar or student does not exist in educational isolation from the dominant culture or white academic world. This is particularly important to understand given how hard it is for black scholars to demonstrate (in some profound way) their abilities and effectiveness as legitimate scholars, with divergent views and political stances. Surely, it is the black scholar's obligation to supply all Americans—or the broad public—with thoughtful explanations of black life, aesthetics and rigorous scholarship. However, black scholars must apply their (brand of) wisdom appropriately to contemporary issues that seem ever changing or dynamic. Furthermore, according to sociologist Nathan Hare, writing in the December 1969 issue of *The Black Scholar*, which is relevant to our discussion:

> The black scholar can no longer afford to ape the allegedly "value free" approach of white scholarship. He must reject absolutely the notion that it is "not professional" ever to become emotional, that it is somehow improper to be "bitter" as a black man, that emotion and reason are mutually exclusive. (1969, p. 61)

Hare, of course, was correct back then about black intellectuals becoming free of their white academic critics, counterparts and detractors. Further, the black scholar today must provide a keen interest in exploring not only traditional approaches and new theories and ideas about what constitute the core curriculum, a controversial subject, or what should be taught, but they must also insist on imparting knowledge about the lives and *aesthetics* of blacks throughout the diasporic world. This in essence means black scholars must use a solid, interdisciplinary approach and all the academic trappings or various means of legitimate scholarship at their disposal when it comes to educational productivity, creativity, and scholarly publishing or whatever academic endeavor they are involved in.

The question again is whether black academics must mimic their white colleagues when it comes to imparting specific knowledge about a subject. And there are, to be sure, subspecialties that the black scholar must also focus on, as many are sometimes taught completely different ways of thinking and learning about a particular topic.

THE WORK OF BLACK SCHOLARS

In years past, the problem for black scholars was not so much a conscious decision to embrace a discipline of black scholarship that would be acceptable to the dominant culture—such as black studies, Pan Africanism, or black history—but this educational myopia or intellectual retrenchment was the only academic game in town at one point in our society (for black scholars). Therefore, confronting the miseducation and intellectual bias from white scholars, of course, was an insult to black scholars everywhere. The gradual movement, of course, from unflattering and open criticism, mistrust, ridicule, and even skepticism by white scholars has been a long road to tread (or 'bridge to breach') for the black scholar, particularly when it comes to writing about a discipline for a scholarly journal and actually publishing. Nevertheless, black scholars, I believe, have finally, or for the most part, conquered that academic hurdle instead of being dismissed or ruthlessly suppressed. Black, Hip-Hop intellectual, and professor of communications, Michael Eric Dyson explains it this way:

> We were subtly but insistently implored to employ the jargon of our disciplines, thereby Black scholars—though this is true for other scholars as well, just not with the same implication about presence or lack of intelligence—are often put in a "damned if you do, damned if you don't bind. On the one hand, we were told for years that our work was worthless, that it lacked the rigor and language by which serious scholarly work is known. Showing our mastery of that plot of intellectual ground we were taught to plow. Then we were told that if our scholarly writings were too jargon-filled they were obtuse and meaningless.
>
> We were told that if we couldn't write in ways that made sense to a broad public our work was of no use. This is good to remember now that critics are taking black public intellectuals to task for our work Back when scholars like Oliver Cox and W.E.B. Du Bois were doing just what it is alleged we often don't do—careful, serious, deeply thoughtful work—they were ignored or dismissed. (Dyson, 1996, p. 64)

A prime example of this almost total lack of attention paid to the works of many black scholars of which Professor Dyson speaks is the relative dismissal by white scholars of well-respected black and historian Lerone Bennett's book, *Forced into Glory: Abraham Lincoln's White Dream*, published by Johnson Publishing Company in 2000. The provocative and discomfiting book argues that "Abraham Lincoln was a racist who kept more blacks in bondage than he ever emancipated" (White, 2000, p. 76). Journalist Jack E. White also writes that Bennett's *Forced into Glory* is "one of the most important reassessments of Lincoln, or any other white figure of similar stature, by a black author." However, it has not gotten "the kind of attention that nonfiction works by white authors have received" (2000, p. 76). And unfortunately, this "ignoring" of black scholars' work will, perhaps, continue, or be a point of contention for the near future.

All in all, however, these things do not change the fact that black scholars are establishing an inordinately large amount of important scholarship, plangent and philosophical insights and scholarly writings that will have a lasting impression and impact on our culture and higher education system. W.E.B. Du Bois' large body of work, for instance, will stand the test of time as a monument to black intellectualism and black aesthetics. Furthermore, many educational officials cogently argue that the quality of black scholars and professors will have the greatest or most impact on black students' achievement, and that is a feat in itself.

In a powerful way, their concerted efforts and work, although not always popular with white academics and higher education officials, has helped black scholars to define themselves in the tough and competitive academic world. Indeed, we must understand that "the United States was a segregated society well up through the 1950s, a place where discourse on race [and black scholarship] was marked by stereotypes and assumptions that bore little resemblance to the lived experience of its black [educated] population" (Naison, 1996, p. 132). This racist frame of thinking and action was especially true about the black scholar in the academe. However, in recent years, many black scholars' views have been remarkably consistent and coherent regarding their status and place in the academy, especially their intellectual pursuits of knowledge, and pedagogy.

WHAT THE BLACK SCHOLAR MUST DO

Moreover, unassailable professionalism in the academy is obviously a double-edged sword, given that some black scholars are not having academic success. Nevertheless, black scholarship has been beyond anybody's expectations recently. In other words, many hard-working black scholars have not reached the academic superstar status—like Afrocentrist, Molefi Kete Asante, Philosopher, Cornel West, Henry Louis Gates, or Bell Hooks—and are still underappreciated. One thing is certain; black scholars of any background can no longer sit on the side lines of the academy jealously looking in or *excluding* themselves from the educational and academic sun, expecting something to happen in their favor. They must *make* things happen in their professional life. Curiously, and to put it bluntly, *many* black scholars have not entered the mainstream of the higher educational and intellectual spectrum and perhaps never will. That is, there are black scholars who will never have parity or achieve full inclusion in the academy or mainstream media for various reasons. Equally important, it must be understood that the brilliant works of many of these black scholars may not change anyone's adverse way of thinking about their scholarship, and newly created diverse, multicultural or revised core curriculums, with black nationalistic kinds of disciplines, such as Afrocentrism or Pan Africanism.

Nonetheless, the black scholar must balance traditional black teachings with contemporary educational challenges, especially in relation to the canon of white scholarship. They must also speak to the passions and struggles of African Americans everywhere, not just in a specific urban or geographical area, which might lead to insights which can be rigorously verified. Toward this end, one must recognize that the heart of the black scholar's work, in the ultimate analysis, should be to tell the truth, to challenge and assist all students, concerned individuals or independent scholars, while empowering them to look at other avenues (novel ways) or unique approaches to thinking and learning new and exciting things, without grasping at straws to make a certain point. Essentially this means that the black scholar must be able to explain and have a better understanding of why such educational complexities and *exigencies* exist in the first place.

Nor must black scholars wear their political and ideological heart on their sleeve to gain some kind of leverage over others. In other words, the black scholar must show an even greater foresight, compassion, and originality in his or her profession, as well as a great suppleness of mind when it comes to competing or participating in academics. Intellectual consistency is also especially important. West explains that "the major obstacle confronting black intellectuals" and the black scholar is:

> the inability to transmit and sustain the requisite institutional mechanisms for the persistence of a discernible intellectual tradition. The racism of American society, the relative lack of black community support, and hence the dangling status of black intellectuals have prevented the creation of a rich heritage of intellectual exchange, intercourse and dialogue. There indeed have been grand black intellectual achievements, but such achievements do not substitute for tradition. (West, 1993, p. 72)

Furthermore, those black scholars who make academic and political arguments based on conventional wisdom or traditional liberalism or liberal ideas will be summarily ignored by influential liberals and conservatives who can quite possibly make a difference in their lives. Therefore, black scholars today must also involve themselves in the politics of the day to challenge the likes of such moderate-liberals as Arthur M. Schlesinger, Jr., and black conservatives, such as economist Thomas Sowell, Supreme Court Justice Clarence Thomas, writer Shelby Steele, or California Board of Regent Ward Connerly, who mistakenly believes that this country is now color blind and 'true equality' exist in all aspects of American life.

By challenging such misguided white liberals and right-wing black conservatives, one can gain different perspectives on current 'hot-button' and cultural issues and intractable American social problems. Indeed, how can black scholars provide a practical understanding of their particular field of study or academic discipline that will be of interest to other intellectuals in American society? No less important, as the eminent black scholar, Nathan Hare has written:

> The black scholar must [still] look beneath the surface of things and, wherever necessary and appropriate, take a stand against the bias of white scholarship. He must be an iconoclast, rallying to the call to arms of all the black intelligentsia, to destroy obsolescent norms and values and create new ones to take their place. (1969, p. 61)

CONCLUSIONS

What is clear is that the black scholar must stay true to himself, regardless of his academic acceptance or nonacceptance by white academical scholars or colleagues. They must also be accurate, consistent, and pragmatic in their scholarship and quest for knowledge; and make important decisions about scientific inquiry and insightful analyses with reasonable certainty about complex outcomes and methodology, especially concerning specific or black nationalistic disciplines. Perhaps most important, the black scholar must avoid at all cost the *arrant* nonsense of pseudo black and white scholarship. More than anything else, the most obvious subject for debate for black scholars is what discipline they will eventually master and teach. At the same time, we must ask: Can black scholars and intellectuals create new academic endeavors or disciplines that might add value and insights to black aesthetics and even the canon of western scholarship?

If one considers, for example, multiculturalism, black feminist studies, and other black nationalist fields of study, like Afrocentricity, as opposed to Eurocentric scholarship, one can clearly ascertain that this is the kind of bold inquiry Professor Hare had in mind in 1969 when he wrote:

> The black scholar must develop new and appropriate norms and values, new institutional structures, and in order to be effective in this regard, he must also

develop and be guided by a new ideology. Out of this new ideology will evolve new methodology, though in some regards it will subsume and overlap existing norms of scholarly endeavor. (1969, p. 62)

The black scholar must also note or recognize they have become (or where they come from) at the beginning of the new millennium or next century. Indeed, what will be the collective influence or impact of the black scholar? Should the black scholar discard the concept of race altogether for a color-blind scholarship, if possible, based on pure scientific inquiry and logic, or continue to embrace racial scholarship that interdicts the forces of racism and White Supremacy? This is to say, must black educators and scholars challenge the dominance of Eurocentric values in education? Moreover, should the black scholar continue to use racial propaganda to insure his or her voice is heard in America? Or can the black intellectual work together collaboratively with white scholars and others to develop solutions to our educational questions and problems of the day by crossing the ideological and racial divide?

Further, and to an unprecedented degree, the black scholars must assist and support each other, without petty jealousies, whenever conceivably possible. This also means, ironically, that they must have a willingness to look at things objectively, as well as provide exclusively young black scholars with mentorship and a means to an end, filling them with promise and hope, so that they might grow as legitimate scholars and intellectuals, which is where it gets complicated. In the end, and through it all, one must finally understand that "the way in which one becomes a black intellectual [or scholar] is highly problematic" (West, 1993, p.68). This is so, according to West, because:

> the traditional roads others travel to become intellectuals in American society have only recently been opened to black people—and remain quite difficult. The main avenues [however] are the academy or the literate subcultures of art, culture and politics. (1993, 0. 68)

Even more important, black scholars must empower themselves by thinking rigorously about big ideas and issues in order to effectively speak and write about hard truths. They must also be able to share these thoughts and important things by getting published and recognized. In this way, the black scholar will contribute to his teaching and education profession, providing the crucial information necessary to decide on any issue, and establishing a sort of pedagogical tradition. A final point worth considering: the black scholar or black practitioners of (new) higher educational disciplines must study systematically the ways of black people in the Diaspora and strike a balance between their own interests, pedagogy, scholarship and professional life. And given these things, the black scholar will give us a greater understanding of our academic world and society.

REFERENCES

Hare, Nathan. 1969, December. "The Challenge Of A Black Scholar." *Black Scholar*.
Naison, Mark D. 1996. "The Significance of the Personal for the Professional." Paul A. Cimbala and Robert F. Himmelberg, editors. *Historians and Race: Autobiography and the Writing of History*. Bloomington and Indianapolis: Indiana University Press.
West, Cornel. 1993. *Keeping Faith: Philosophy and Race in America*. New York: Routledge.
White, Jack E. 2000, May. "Was Lincoln A Racist?" *Time*.

Reflections on Revisionist History and Scientific Racism

INTRODUCTION

After reading several articles about African Americans in a major southwestern newspaper, I was compelled to write to an editor for the first time in my entire life. The first newspaper article was concerning Alexander Cockburn's commentary, "Juries Were in Process of Nullifying Slavery," a critique of Godfrey D. Lehman's 1998 book, *We The Jury,* which asserts that the U.S. Courts system would have ended slavery. The other short article was about a misinformed white college instructor's insistence that blacks, brutally taken from their African lands, actually enjoyed being slaves and didn't want to be liberated by the so-called Yankees during the Civil War. The instructor was teaching an *incorrect* and revisionist American or civil war history (for credit) at a community college in North Carolina. (Fortunately, the course was eventually eliminated from the college curriculum after much protest from local blacks and the NAACP.)

Both of these articles, of course, were filled with historical inaccuracies, egalitarian myths, and misstatements (or false interpretations or misinterpretations). I might point out that I am a black scholar, and as I teach American Politics and African American history, I discussed the aforementioned articles and work with some of my academic colleagues and students. They agreed with my intellectual assessments. Therefore, I was determined to set the record straight—at least with this local newspaper—about these issues. Hence, I wrote the editor of the newspaper. I was forewarned, however, that this particular newspaper rarely permitted a liberal voice to be heard.

But I was unconvinced. So I submitted a lengthy letter regarding my concerns to the editor anyway. A couple of days later, the editor of the newspaper surprisingly called me and indicated that he wanted to publish my letter, but he asked me if I could delete the extensive quotes and shorten the piece to one, single-spaced page. I told the editor that I was not inclined to change *anything* about my letter because I had read even longer Op-ed (or editorial page) pieces from different professors in the paper.

I finally told the editor that if he wanted to change the piece (my letter) for publication, it was fine with me—that is, as long as he didn't change or *obliterate* the point I was trying to make.

Needless to say, the editor *never* published the letter. I was finally convinced that my (Jewish) colleague was right about the intrepid Midwestern newspaper, which seems to support an ultra-conservative, right wing or far-right viewpoint. It is important to consider that historically, minorities have rarely had a voice in the white conservative press. Perhaps this is so because "ethnic groups and people of color are not numerical minorities in many societies, and whites are a minority in the world population" (Schwartz, 1995, p. 44).

In either case, I now understand that this biased position by many newspaper editors, white owners, and staunch conservative gatekeepers is the unfortunate rule, not the exception. As a result, minorities are not fully given their due in the white news media. In fact, I personally believe that the media perpetuate some of the racial problems that we have in the United States.

In the end, I was undeterred in my dealings with the newspaper editor and decided to include the information that I wrote him in this particular chapter because it tries to objectively point out the truth of these contentious matters.

THE PROBLEM WITH SCIENTIFIC RACISM

From the outset then, it must be clearly understood that our society is like a festering wound that cannot quite heal. Nor will we ever heal our nation's problems regarding race and the enduring issues of American slavery and race if we are given (or presented with) a distorted and one-sided or slanted version of sociology, philosophy, and American history—that is, just to appease a few white Southerners and racist bigots who are still living in the past.

For example, some whites in the South continue to portray or re-enact their ancestors' (failed) part in the Civil War; and they are still resisting what they call "a Yankee invasion" of their southern home land. Why, I wonder, are they still fighting this battle? Perhaps some white Southerners wished they had won. Yes, we must remember the lessons of our past and fragile history, but that history should not be distorted to accommodate the biased, and scientific racism evident in such recent academic studies done by white intellectual supremacists, such as in the late Richard J. Herrnstein and Charles Murray's book, *The Bell Curve*, which tries to prove that blacks are genetically inferior to all other races; and Godfrey D. Lehman's *We The Jury*, a revisionist and "what if" account of American slave history.

In a nutshell, we must remember that these pseudo-historical and scientific books "are not written for the sake of any science [or historical truths], as they are created for political reasons" (Brown, 1995, p. 99). Therefore, there is nothing new about their lame argument or brand of virulent racism. Just before *The Bell Curve* was published, African American journalist and syndicated radio talk-show host, Tony Brown, wrote that co-authors Herrnstein and Murray believed that:

> Welfare programs, affirmative action, Head Start, and any other efforts to help elevate the lives of the American underclass have been a waste of time because Blacks are genetically flawed. In fact, the unstated implication is that Blacks in general are a waste of time. And that, of course, officially marginalizes an entire race of people. This makes Black candidates for eventual extermination, at least to anyone who has studied the history of genocide or triage. (1995, p. 96)

Even more important, as white political scientist Andrew Hacker tells us, Herrnstein and Murray ardently believe that "our places are ordered by our genetic capacities, and persons of African ancestry should accept their limitations and settle for less demanding callings" (1995, p. 49). This prejudicial counsel by Herrnstein and Murray is the typical or common racist theme evoked by white intellectual racists throughout the world. And I suspect that many whites feel this way in the United States, also. But are they afraid to voice their true feelings out loud because this would be a politically incorrect thing to do today? Herrnstein and Murray go on to conclude that "Instead of aiming for Ivy League colleges and corner offices, they [blacks] should hone their talents for the kinds of occupations their forebears followed" (Hacker, 1995, p. 49). This in essence, means blacks should be satisfied with menial roles and occupations.

The blatant racism promulgated by Herrnstein and Murray is absolutely shameful, but not without precedent. For an interesting discussion of how and why white racists have been able to perpetuate the myth of racial superi-

ority, one should read ethnologist Michael Bradley's *The Iceman Inheritance*.
According to Bradley's bold and controversial thesis:

> The so-called 'white race' is more aggressive, more violent, than other human
> groups. It is also more prone to sexism and racism. This lamentable
> predilection is due to the 'iceman inheritance,' i.e., genetic contamination by a
> race of people whose character was traumatically determined by the merciless
> conditions of the ice age. (1978, p. xii)

Although Bradley is an amateur in the field, and doesn't provide a shred
of plausible anthropological evidence, many black scholars are sometimes
inclined to agree with his bold and farfetched premise, because *intuitively*, and
in some respects, they perhaps believe he might be partly correct. Nonetheless, Hacker goes on to point out that the authors of *The Bell Curve* maintain
that "descendants of slaves would be well advised to repress any feelings they
have of entitlement or envy. [And] if that attitude can be brought about, we
would be a happy and stable society, much like a modern version of an
antebellum plantation" (Hacker, 1995, p. 49).

What rubbish. Herrnstein and Murray are essentially saying that blacks
should accept subordination and be in some kind of *servitude* or (even perhaps) slavery to whites who are supposedly superior. According to the brilliant
African American psychologist, Brent Staples, "The idea that some groups
are genetically superior to others is the most poisonous notion in the history
of civilization. [And] if you doubt that, think again. It was the claim of Aryan
superiority that led to the Nazi extermination of six million Jews" (Staples,
1995, p. 113). The fact of the matter is that such absurd beliefs are all about a
revival of (racist) eugenic thought by those who think the world would be
better off with only the white human group. Writes Tony Brown:

> This sort of thinking holds that social programs have failed and the Black
> underclass has only grown larger because Blacks are intellectually inferior because
> of genetic makeup. There is nothing that can be done for this genetically
> inferior class of people, and so nothing should be done for them—as this
> revived line of eugenic thought goes. (1995, p. 98).

All in all, the authors of *The Bell Curve* present an unacceptable and racist
message. Staples, for example, contends that "the book belabors the point
that on average Blacks score lower on IQ tests than Whites. But enlightened
scientists know that difference is due to environment and experience" (1995,
p. 113). Staples is absolutely right on this point, but I would add: So what?

Indeed, what does this have to do with blacks in the greater scheme of things, and whether or not they can survive in a racist society, dominated by white Americans? One must understand that in a racist society, Pandora's Box will always be opened regarding the issues of genetics and race relations. And there is no way of getting around that.

Put another way by Fischer and other sociologists at the Department of Sociology at the University of California at Berkeley:

> The test of intelligence Herrnstein and Murray use, and most others, too, really measure how much academic instruction people have had, not their inherent abilities. Even if such tests did measure differences in native intelligence, those differences do *not* explain very much about inequality among individuals in America, individuals' social environments explain more. (1996, p. 171)

If Fischer and others are right, one has to believe that the remedy for the Black underclass is better education. (Staples, 1995, p. 113) Staples believes, moreover, that Herrnstein and Murray had a more sinister purpose in mind when they wrote *The Bell Curve*, because "without a shred of plausible evidence, they argue [as already intimated by Brown] that intelligence is so wired into genes that *nothing* can be done to improve the minds of the [black] poor" (Staples, 1995, p. 143).

This notion by Herrnstein and Murray, however, is utter nonsense, because African Americans have been able to improve their lot in life or terrible plight in the United States (considerably) by the opportunities of education, and by improving their particular environments, or where they reside. Staples reasons that what Herrnstein and Murray are "really about is justifying the status quo and lending a veneer of science to social inequality" (Staples, 1995, p. 113). And as there has been no real or strong objection by conservatives in the academic community, one has to believe that they tacitly approved the nonsense or mumbo jumbo in *The Bell Curve*, as well as the inequality or inferiority of blacks. More significantly, as Fischer and others have accurately asserted and explained:

> The distribution of individual intelligence has little to do with the extent of inequality in a society; patterns of inequality are produced by the economic and social structures of the nation and era. Both the conditions that help or impede individuals' race to succeed and the system of inequality within which those individuals compete are heavily governed by social policies. Thus, policy choices have shaped the kind of class inequality we have. Policy choices, over the long course of American history, have shaped the kind of racial inequality we have, as well. (Fischer & Et.al., 1996, p. 171)

In the ultimate analysis, and "in such an atmosphere of racial conscious-ness, it becomes increasingly difficult to construct any national identity" (Wilkinson, 1997, p. 27). Staples finally writes that "the latest infestation of scientific racism as seen in *The Bell Curve* is but one more twist on an old and dangerous theme. African-Americans need to master that theme and stand ready to defend themselves against it" (Staples, 1995, p. 113). If blacks do not defend against these racist themes, and bogus social scientists, I believe they will be adversely *subjected* to them in the future, and perhaps to their detriment.

THE MISUSES OF HISTORY AND ABUSES OF HISTORICAL RACISM

As an African American, descendant of black slaves, author, former U.S. Army colonel, and now college professor, I was personally offended by a recent commentary made by columnist Alexander Cockburn, which claimed that "slavery might have been resolved peaceably through trials by jury—without war." Cockburn reached this dubious conclusion after reading Godfrey D. Lehman's *We The Jury*. Cockburn's assessments, of course, are ridiculous, since black slaves did not have a voice in the American political court systems at that time. Indeed, had it not been for the Civil War, perhaps black Ameri-cans would still be enslaved in some way. Professors, respectively of history and law, Mary Frances Berry and John W. Blassingame have written:

> From the beginning of their history in the United States, blacks raised critical issues concerning the criminal justice system: procedural fairness in trials of blacks, the inequalities in administration of justice (from arrest to sentencing after trial to post conviction remedies), the punishment of whites for mistreatment of blacks, and the sentences blacks and whites received for the same offense. (Berry & Blassingame, 1982, p. 228)

Furthermore, black slaves were considered property, like a horse or cattle, and were not given citizenship until Congress and the respective States (rightly) ratified the Fourteenth Amendment to the Constitution. Second, slaves could not serve on white juries, particularly in the South, or even testify against whites in many courts of law throughout the United States. Berry and Blassingame explain it this way:

> Southern free Negroes generally were not permitted to testify in cases involving whites. They did, however...win suits for property or freedom from the appellate courts. The judges did not seem to regard decisions favorable to

blacks as a threat to slavery. However, the specific social and economic circumstances of the black litigants and ties to some white protector in the community were major factors in the successful suits. (1982, p. 35)

Therefore, a few isolated cases in northern courts that may or may not have benefited slaves did not destroy the awful and peculiar institution of slavery in America. As Cockburn and Godfrey D. Lehman should very well know, black slaves were being maimed for constantly running away, sexually abused and assaulted, terrorized and brutally beaten into submission—to work for mostly white slave holders. Cockburn also talks about what happened essentially in the courts of Massachusetts and other mostly northern states, not what occurred in the South. Moreover, it must be understood that "on the national level, federal law excluded free Negroes from militia service and excluded blacks from carrying the U.S. mail. Federal lawmakers also authorized the citizens of Washington, D.C., to elect only white city officials and to adopt a code governing free Negroes and slaves and denied passports to free Negroes" (Berry & Blassingame, 1982, p. 35).

In other words, the court cases that ruled in favor of blacks in the North did not establish any precedent for the South, where the laws concerning blacks were more stringent. There we find the outright lynching or murder of *recalcitrant* slaves, the institution of harsh slave code laws and later black code laws, which limited blacks in almost every aspect of their daily lives.

We must also understand that, without a doubt, "Cotton was King" in the Southern States, and white slave owners did *everything* in their power to perpetrate and maintain the profitable system of slavery, to include denying blacks their constitutional rights, such as the right of suffrage or franchise after the Civil War and Reconstruction. Some Southern legislatures even enacted laws to reenslave freed blacks, as occurred in Tennessee in 1857 and Texas in 1859, as well as in other Southern slave-holding states. As the late Judge and Harvard Law professor, A. Leon Higginbotham, Jr. has written:

In the United States, segregated courthouse restrooms, cafeterias, and spectator seating...acted as signals. In these cases all participants, particularly juries in criminal or civil trials involving an African American defendant or litigant, were constantly reminded that African Americans were to be accorded inferior status in this society. Every time jurors and spectators walked into a courtroom, they were presented with a ringing affirmation of the assumptions, myths, and attitudes that compose the ideology of racism in the United States. (Higginbotham, 1996, p. 130)

Even more important, with the lucrative free labor from black slaves, white antebellum juries were not in the process of nullifying slavery or accommodating blacks in any humane way if they could possibly help it. To think otherwise is a distortion of history and the truth. White pseudo-scholars, however, would have us believe that blacks enjoyed their captivity, as suggested in a 1998 article in the *Las Vegas Review Journal.* According to that article, "slaves were happy in captivity and that many served as loyal Southern soldiers" (College Course, 1998, p. 9A). Nothing could be further from the truth, however.

Professor of History at Stanford University, Kennell Jackson in his insightful 1996 book, *America Is Me,* writes "Black slaves often wore a mask. Out of necessity, they disguised their true feelings, hid their resistance, feigned humility, and deferred [overwhelmingly] to their masters and mistresses" (1996, p. 87). Jackson also pragmatically points out that slaves lied to themselves in order to live. (1996, p. 87)

This is to say, if you were a poor, illiterate black slave, threatened with an agonizing death or some other horrible repercussions every day of your life for trying to read or write—or even to understand the essence of things (or related affairs)—whom would you believe if you heard nothing else beside what the 'Slave Master' told you or wanted you to hear? Imagine knowing no other life, no other existence. I think it is fair to say that slaves deplored their miserable existence, and they did not willingly embrace their conditions of servitude. Quite the contrary. Many slaves had been mentally and psychologically whipped, or had given up all hope in some cases, so they grudgingly accepted their lot in life.

In earnest, we must understand and recognize that black slaves were being coerced and spoon-fed egregious lies and falsehoods, because of their illiteracy, ignorance, and limited knowledge about the Civil War and the so-called "Evil Empire of the North." Obviously, an academician such as Jack Perdue of Randolph Community College in North Carolina, who is cited earlier, did not do his homework. And apparently he (Perdue) never read *From Slavery To Freedom,* the landmark work of the eminent African American historian, John Hope Franklin. Franklin writes:

> One of the greatest anxieties of the South at the beginning of the war was the conduct of slaves. The reaction of slaves to their status involved not only the security of the white civilian population but also the maintenance of a stable economic system without which there was no hope of prosecuting the war successfully. [And] gradually slaves became aware that in this war their freedom was at stake. (1994, p. 209)

And slaves certainly wanted to be free, despite words to the contrary. Perhaps if Perdue had read Franklin's monumental work, he might really have learned something about how black slaves actually felt about their cursed captivity. Many slaves, in fact, *were* looking to the North for their salvation. Perdue and other white southerners should just read some of the many slave narratives, such as Solomon Northup's *Twelve Years A Slave* or *The Interesting Narrative of the Life of Olaudah Equiano* for their accounts about the harsh realities of their enslavement, instead of selectively writing about black history without challenge.

I was deeply offended and outraged that such a pseudo-course in Southern History was even taught at Randolph Community College. Moreover, after a second reading, I noted that the course was offered and taught by local members of the Sons of Confederate Veterans. That quickly explained things for me. Indeed, what could one expect from such a polarizing and parochial group? We must all consider the source. Ultimately, offering such a deceptive college course, disguised as a scholarly and academic endeavor, is evidence of the kind of 'narrow-minded' thinking that is typical of pseudo-scholars and educators who would try to re-write our history. Moreover, it supports the racist or white supremacist notions that blacks are inferior and sub-human and that slaves were content with their degrading, wretched, and subordinate position in life.

Analyzing the interviews of former slaves and reaching such a biased and narrow-minded conclusion is ridiculous, and not particularly scientific. Besides, how did those white interviewers know what these former slaves really felt? More importantly, what did these so-called interviewers expect these former slaves to say to the same faces as their primary and former oppressors and tormentors? Were they afraid to speak the truth because of some fear of retribution? I think so. Additionally, the assertion that slaves relished their captivity is, of course, a fabrication. Otherwise, why did white Southerners fear the idea of blacks learning how to read and write—and fear the very thought of black uprisings, where white slave-owners would be summarily massacred? In fact, on many slave plantations, blacks outnumbered their white masters and overseers.

Moreover, why did we have several slave uprisings—such as with Denmark Vesey's 1822 conspiracy, and Gabriel Prosser's attack on Richmond, Virginia, or Nat Turner's rebellion in Southampton, Virginia, where approximately 60 whites were slain—if slaves were satisfied with being slaves? Were these slaves "outsiders" trying to stir up the masses of supposedly docile and obedient blacks? Absolutely not. Nat Turner was a mystical black preacher who taught himself how to write and read the Bible; and through a reported vision, he decided, along with other trusted slaves allies, that enough was enough. That meant Turner thought slavery should end *immediately*. Many slaves, of course, felt that way.

Political correctness (or the so-called current "diversity" dogma) is not even part of the historical equation, nor does it have anything to do with some of these inaccurate accounts presented by pseudo-scholars and their sometimes racist bent on twisting the facts. So what if 38,000 blacks fought in the Confederate Army, as Professor Perdue points out? You can perhaps triple the number of freed blacks and former slaves who fought for the Union Army. In fact, many escaped, ran away to the North, and joined the fight against the Confederates. Some questions, however, remain: Were the slaves coerced or forced into serving the Confederate Armies? Or did these 38,000 blacks volunteer? According to Civil War scholar Richard Rollins, "Black Southerners gave support to both sides, and that support was conditional, based on individual assessments of the situation at hand. For the majority, the war brought not elation and joy but anxiety, wariness, and difficult choices: (Rollins, 1994, p. 5).

Moreover, what kind of military jobs were blacks given while serving in the Confederate Army? Were there any black generals or officers who led white soldiers into battle? Were black slaves given command of Confederate troops? No. Absolutely not. Most of those blacks who served the Confederacy, mind you, served in menial roles, such as bootblacks, blacksmiths, horse attendants, waiters, and cooks. Rollins ventures that, "Black Southerners found their way into combat in Confederate Armies in three ways, but perhaps the largest numbers were the ubiquitous "body servants" (1994, p. 9). In other words, white Confederate soldiers depended on blacks to do the hard and dirty work.

Also, not too many blacks were given rifles or arms because many white confederates feared a backlash, that their "gun-carrying" slaves would perhaps turn these weapons against them—their former slave-masters. Famous Civil War historian James M. McPherson has accurately asserted that:

> Wedded to the ideologies of slavery and Negro subordination, the Confederacy was incapable of treating [free blacks] fairly or justly, even when [they] volunteered [their] support for the Confederate cause. Southern leaders suspected, with good reason, that the real loyalties of most Southern [Blacks] lay with the North. During the war most Confederate states enacted restrictive and repressive legislation against free [blacks], the purpose of which was to keep them under constant surveillance and in a condition closely resembling slavery. (1965, p. 24)

More significantly, regarding the suitability of blacks' serving as soldiers, "there was opposition from Confederates who questioned whether [blacks] serving as soldiers could be returned to slavery after the war and who would work the region's farms if slaves were taken away" (Role of Black Confederates, 1999, p. 7A).

Equally important, "there's little indication that any all-black Confederate units went to war" (Role of Black Confederates, 1999, p. 7A). Finally, there was no true loyalty among slaves, only their fear of the white master's boot and whip on their backs, as well as other forms of violence and atrocities, if they did not obey or acquiesce. One, however, must also remember that loyalty was a two-way street. And white slave-holders were rarely loyal to their slaves. According to John Hope Franklin and Moss, "the most widespread form of disloyalty [by black slaves] was desertion" (Franklin & Moss, 1994, p. 209). Franklin and Moss go on to outline the disloyalty of slaves when he pointed out that "almost the entire slave population of the Shirley plantation in Virginia deserted to the Union lines. Moreover, in August 1862, a Confederate general estimated that slaves worth at least $1 million were escaping to the federals in North Carolina" (Franklin & Moss, 1994, p. 209).

Furthermore, "the truth of the matter is," as Tamara Baker of St. Paul, Minnesota, correctly tells us in a July 1999 letter to the editors of *USA Today*:

> While General Robert E. Lee had for months asked that the Confederacy be allowed to force black slaves to fight alongside white rebels, the Congress of the Confederacy, facing vehement opposition from slave owners, only approved the idea in March 28, 1865—a bare two weeks before the end of the war and far too late to be implemented. (Baker, 1999, p. 12A)

When revisionists and pseudo-scholars, who have written history about blacks in an unflattering way in the past, try to write and publish these myths and falsehoods—that is, to twist historical events to suit their particular needs and political agenda in order to glorify their ancestors' involvement in the Civil War and slavery—it flies in the face of precise history and our multiracial democracy. Civil War historian Richard Rollins cogently explains that:

> Just as surely as we have been misled by Southern writers before, during and after the war who propagated and endorsed the "myth of the happy slave" to support their view of slavery as a benign institution, we have apparently just begun to comprehend the minds and hearts of black Southerners during the [civil] war, and to study and understand how they truly felt about it, and how the war actually affected their lives. (Rollins, 1994, p. 5)

In so many words, influential white intellectual supremacists who use anecdotal accounts and evidence (like Murray, Herrnstein, and Lehman) should be ashamed of themselves, because they, as well as others, are in denial about our inglorious history and tragic past. Perhaps the Sons of Confederate Veterans or many white Southerners today just can't handle the bitter past and truth. After all, the South *decisively* lost its so-called War for Southern Independence.

Finally, why should anyone have pride in a treasonous rabble of individuals who committed egregious crimes against innocent people and our great nation? Moreover, should we not consider many of these Confederates as traitors? Many descendants of white Confederates say that it was a right of Southerners to self-determination, but this is just senseless talk. Wasn't it really an outright treasonous rejection of our remarkable Constitution? Any group that tried to violate the sovereignty of our national government today would be swiftly put down and prosecuted.

My personal advice to those revisionist scholars (as well as their descendants) who are still living in the distant past because of their political socialization is: Get over it. That is, get rid of your hatred and (personal) prejudices if you possibly can. This is the only way, I believe, we can solve our intractable problems of race in many American communities and survive as a nation. Otherwise, we are dooming ourselves and our existence on this planet, and more importantly, our survival as the human race.

REFERENCES

Baker, Tamara. 1999, July 7. "There never were any 'Black Confederate Soldiers.'" *USA Today*.

Berry, Mary F. & Blassingame, John W. 1982. *Long Memory: The Black Experience in America*. New York: Oxford University Press.

Bradley, Michael. 1978. *The Iceman Inheritance: Prehistoric Sources of Western Man's Racism, Sexism and Aggression*. New York: Warner Books, Inc.

Brown, Tony. 1995. *Black Lies, White Lies: The Truth According to Tony Brown*. New York: William Morrow and Company, Inc.

"College Course on Slaves Irks Blacks." 1998, November 16. *Las Vegas Review Journal*.

Fischer, Claude S., Hout, Michael, Jankowski, Martin S., Lucas, Sammuel R., Swidler, Ann, & Voss, Kim. 1996. *Inequality by Design: Cracking the Bell Curve Myth*. Princeton, New Jersey: Princeton University Press.

Franklin, John H. & Moss, Alfred A. Jr. 1994. *From Slavery to Freedom: A History of African Americans*. 7th edition. New York: McGraw-Hill, Inc.

Hacker, Andrew. 1995, July 10. "The crackdown on African-Americans." *The Nation.*

Higginbotham, A. Leon, Jr. 1996. *Shades of Freedom: Racial Politics and Presumptions of the American Legal Process.* New York: Oxford University Press.

Jackson, Kennell. 1996. *America Is Me: 170 Fresh Questions and Answers on Black American History.* New York: Harper Collins.

McPherson, James M. 1965. *The Negro's Civil War: How American Negroes Felt and Acted During the War for the Union.* New York: Vintage Books. Note also that McPherson points out that blacks served in the Confederacy mainly because of "local patriotism and the hope of better treatment. But there is also evidence that pressure from local [white] officials and fear of impressment played a part in the decision of some Southern [Blacks] to volunteer" (p. 24).

"Role of Black Confederates Questioned." 1999, February 21. *Las Vegas Review Journal.*

Rollins, Richard. editor. 1994. *Black Southerners in Gray: Essays on Afro-Americans in Confederate Armies.* Redondo Beach, California: Rank and File Publications.

Schwartz, Marilyn. 1995. *Guidelines for Bias-Free Writing.* Bloomington: Indiana University Press.

Staples, Brent. 1995, January. "This is Not A Test." *Essence Magazine.*

Wilkinson, J. Harvie, III. 1977. *One Nation Indivisible: How Ethnic Separatism Threatens America.* Reading Massachusetts: Addison-Wesley Publishing Company, Inc.

The Pragmatism of Francis Fukuyama: Exploring Black Studies, Multiculturalism, and Liberalism in American Society

MEGALOTHYMIA AND THE DIRECTIONALITY OF HISTORY

Throughout the history of mankind, there have always been those (with racist minds and attitudes) who have maintained the idea of superiority of one race over another. For instance, in the 1800s, the British naturalist Charles Darwin proposed the theory of "Survival of the Fittest," especially, I believe, of Anglo Saxon whites in the world. This notion by Darwin, of course, simply means that it was/is only right and proper that the strongest and most powerful rule the day in all things, no matter the situation, circumstances, or eventualities.

Darwin's philosophy invariably raises the question of *genocide*, which means the systematic destruction and annihilation of a particular race of people and their specific civilization. Unfortunately, throughout the existence of mankind, *genocide* has been considered the *accepted* progression of life, by racists, in terms of natural selection, and supposedly the right order of things. Writing about the genocide of blacks, slavery, and the general destruction of the peoples of Africa, for example, Afrocentrist theorist Chancellor Williams in his widely speculative book, *The Destruction of Black Civilization*, has inquired:

How was this highly advanced Black Civilization so completely destroyed that its people, in our times and for some centuries past, have found themselves not only behind the other peoples of the world, but as well, the color of their skin a sign of inferiority, bad luck, and the badge of the slave whether bond or free? And, since...whites were once enslaved as generally as any other race, how did it come about that slavery was finally concentrated in Africa on blacks only?

The different dark-skinned races or human species of color on this planet, however, have been able to survive the *inevitable* onslaught of perhaps their extinction, despite the destructiveness, persecution, terrible brutality and the inhumaneness wrought against them by others. Nonetheless, we must remember that we are all basically from the same stuff or source of life, despite our differences or various racial, religious and cultural groups and political ideologies. And no so-called race is innately superior. Therefore, the closest thing to the term *megalothymia*, as mentioned in the introductory title to this chapter, is the idea or notion of *ethnocentrism*, which has been defined by the political historian, James MacGregor Burns (1995, p. 185 and p. G4) as:

> A selective perception based on individual background, attitudes, and biases that leads one to believe in the superiority of one's nation or ethnic group.

But the term "megalothymia" means more than Burns' explanation of ethnocentrism. According to political theorist Francis Fukuyama, writing in his provocative, controversial, and scintillating book, *The End of History and the Last Man*, it also means "a desire to be recognized as superior to other people" (Fukuyama, 1993, p. 182). Even more important, as Fukuyama (1993, p. 182) goes on to write:

> *Megalothymia* can be manifested both in the tyrant who invades and enslaves a neighboring people so that they will recognize his authority, as well as in the concert pianist who wants to be recognized as the foremost interpreter of Beethoven.

Fukuyama also cogently discusses the term "isothymia," which is the desire to be recognized as the equal of other people" (Zinn, 1990, p. 36). This definition is also important to note because blacks in the United States (and elsewhere in the Diaspora) have tried to prove relentlessly and *unequivocally* that they are the equal to the vast American majority or dominant white group and other peoples of the world. For example, in the late 1960s, black scholars and historians tried to establish their *isothymia* by introducing Black Aesthetics and Black Studies programs at many White American universities. Professor Howard Zinn writes:

> These multiplying black studies programs [did] not pretend to just introduce another subject for academic inquiry. They [had] the specific intention of so affecting the consciousness of black and white people in this country as to diminish for both groups the pervasive American belief in black *inferiority*. (1990, p. 36)

Black people—although historically underprivileged and underrepresented in the fledgling industrial work force during the first part of the twentieth century, and particularly at elite white colleges and universities and other higher educational institutions—later proved to be the equal to whites and all other peoples—in many ways—in the world. Nonetheless, Black Studies in the United States has yet to *equalize* things *economically* or *educationally* for African Americans. Perhaps the discipline was never designed to accomplish that task. Using a scholarly perspective, and according to Professor Robert S. Boynton (1995, p. 64):

> The birth of black studies was a particularly important development, because it provided the institutional as well as the intellectual power base that would later prove helpful when black intellectuals began teaching at the elite [white] universities they had attended. This was the first generation of black scholars to progress almost entirely outside traditionally black institutions like Howard and Morehouse, and it adopted a more optimistic attitude toward the possibilities afforded by an academic life.

The question here, however, is why many of these black scholars and black intellectuals didn't *champion* the study of aesthetics, Black Studies and Multiculturalism fully in the core college curriculum, rather than accepting totally a *eurocentric* core? Indeed, can there ever be a balance in the varied subjects (or disciplines) that we teach at the university and higher educational level? Yes, new multicultural ideas as well as teaching the Great Works must be embraced for the sake of learning. But we must also incorporate the modern-day multicultural works in order for us to be more effective and more equal (and complete) in our pedagogy.

Equally important, we must understand that if the conservative cultural traditionalists had it their way, all manner of multicultural enterprises would be eliminated. According to former U.S. Secretary of Education and staunch conservative Republican, William Bennett (1998, p. 25):

Some [liberal educators even] argue that our nation's cultural and ethnic diversity makes it impossible to construct a core curriculum appropriate for all students and schools. [He goes on]: They may concede that *curricular* deterioration is a problem, but they resist the obvious solution, believing instead that our sprawling, heterogeneous culture defies any attempt to codify an American 'canon' of essential learning.

What the reactionary Bennett is really saying here, I believe, is that separate racial and ethnic (educational) enclaves on American campuses—in order to equalize things—is a false idea or promise, and would promote suspicion, mistrust and a sort of hatred if you will on the part of many white students, administrators and faculty members.

I think what Bennett and other opponents must recognize, though, is that without such disciplines as Black Studies or Ethnic Studies, minorities who attend these elite white institutions will continue to be concerned, less trusting, and suspicious of the dominant culture. Furthermore, a lack of knowledge of multicultural works does limit our experiences and knowledge about the world and other educational matters? Indeed, if we are limited in what we can ask, does this not limit our ability to *know*, to learn new ways of thinking and teaching, which would *allow us* to bring a positive sense of challenge and wonder to the canon of scholarship?

Contrary to what has been written by Bennett, conservative demagogues and other fierce opponents—university faculties, multiculturalists, and other minority administrators—at higher educational institutions, in most cases (and unfortunately), have very little to say about exercising *full* control over the core college curricula.

Toward this end, as Fukuyama (1993, p. 183) has so astutely pointed out, "the *megalothymia* of would-be masters to dominate other people through imperialism was an important theme in a good deal of medieval and early modern political thought, which referred to the phenomenon as the quest for glory."

Additionally, we must realize that the idea of *megalothymia* has historically been used to *dehumanize* dark-skinned people and the entire black race, not just blacks in America, but in the entire Diaspora. Perhaps because of this, we should now *glorify* Black Studies, multiculturalism, Black Feminism, and aesthetics, to the extent that all students must learn about these important educational matters. Indeed, let's make learning such things an *innate* graduation requirement at all colleges and universities in the United States.

This would be an important step in bridging the racial divide, because in the past, and shortly after Reconstruction, there was almost no glory or hope for blacks in the United States until the initial eradication of legal segregation, or the 'separate-but-equal' doctrine, commonly known as the Plessy v. Ferguson decision. Perhaps the birth of this eradication effectively took place in 1948 in the United States Armed Forces—that is, when President Harry Truman issued an executive order integrating all branches of the military services. Stephen Budiansky (1993, p. 42) adds:

> In carrying out President Truman's 1948 executive order directing "equality of treatment" for all members of the armed forces, the military—playing a role still not widely recognized—arguably did more than *any* other institution in American to bring down the nation's racial barriers.

And despite Truman's prejudicial or white *superiority* bent, he initiated important federal policies that tried to improve the lot and livelihood of all African Americans. But this hope for equality by black Americans in the middle part of the twentieth century was short lived. Sociologist Harvard Sitkoff (1971, p. 614) writes:

> Although the *euphoric* hopes of Negroes [blacks] proved premature in Truman's second administration, the campaign of 1948 [was] a milestone in the coming of age of the civil rights issue. For the first time since Reconstruction, civil rights occupied a central place on the political stage. Never before had so many written and said so much about the Negro's right to equality. Going beyond the usual promises of patronage and lucrative advertising contracts, both national [political] parties and the *Progressives* competed for the Negro (or Black) vote by stressing their concern for civil rights.

Blacks in America, however, would have to wait another five decades to even reach a semblance of true equality. Even to this day, the playing field or *parity* for blacks—socially and politically—still hasn't been fully achieved or realized. This has not been from a lack of trying on the part of Pan-Africanists, Black nationalists, Afrocentric scholars and Black dilettantes, as well as Black politicians and Black academics and public intellectuals. In fact, the modern-day black nationalist movement in the guise of Afrocentrism has maintained the struggle of blacks to achieve true equality in the United States—at least educationally and economically.

TOWARD A DEFINITION OF FUKUYAMA'S AFROCENTRISM

It may or may not be astonishing to know that Fukuyama's work is not about *Afrocentrism* in and of itself. That is, at no point does Fukuyama explain in detail about the superiority of one ethnic group over the other. Fukuyama's book, *The End of History and The Last Man*, however, does briefly deal with the complicated 'social-struggle' issues of blacks in the *Diaspora*—that is, blacks in America and elsewhere in the world, other than in Africa, especially in his prophetic and pragmatic discussion of humankind and history. As Fukuyama chronicles and analyzes past (historical) events, for example, he is extremely adept in telling us that, "despite the abolishment of legally sanctioned barriers to equality in the 1960s…and the rise of a variety of affirmative action programs [supposedly] giving preference to blacks, a certain sector of the American black population [has] not only failed to advance economically, but [they have] actually lost ground" (Fukuyama, 1993, p. 237). Fukuyama, I believe, is specifically referring to poor blacks, not the black middle classes.

It is extremely important to understand what he is saying, but it is also significant because, 'white supremacy,' I believe, is the real problem in the world today; and it still reigns supreme in America—that is, one group of people continue to have power and authority over blacks and all other minorities in the United States—and this is why ending racism and discrimination in this country, and throughout the world, will never be an easy task to accomplish. Perhaps it is an impossible task.

Some would even go so far as to say that racism and the severe disadvantages of black Americans and perhaps other minorities will never end. This is especially true in the United States, because we are still debating, for example, whether or not blacks are *genetically* and *intellectually* inferior to all other races, or even if they deserve affirmative action or racial preferences. Consequently, Fukuyama (1993, p. 237) goes on to write that:

> Rather than seeking integration in a color-blind society, some black leaders stress instead the need to take pride in a distinct Afro-American culture with its own history, traditions, heroes, and values, equal to but separate from the culture of white society. In some cases this shades over into an "Afro-centrism" which asserts the superiority of indigenous African culture over "European" ideas like socialism and capitalism.

The brilliant black newspaper journalist and scholar, Sam Fulwood (1995, p. 1D) might agree with Fukuyama's assertion that blacks have not generally made much progress in America, basically because of the institutionalization and *indignities* of racism and 'white supremacy.' Fulwood writes that:

> A growing body of evidence suggest that in the wake of a series of tense incidents that have high-lighted racial disparities, the willingness of large numbers of black Americans to work as hard as they once did for a color-blind society is receding. (1995, p. 10)

In a large sense, this rolling back of the *multicultural* ideals has occurred because of the continuing economic disparities and racist confrontations that go on in the United States today; for example, the notion of racial profiling—or DWB (Driving While Black)—is still prevalent in our society today. This means blacks are stopped by local law enforcement officials solely based on the color of their skin. Therefore, in a nutshell, many blacks are suggesting 'isolationism' or segregation again from white society rather than integration—period. There is no doubt, as pointed out by the Afrocentric scholar Molefi Kete Asante, that this re-segregation is occurring because black Americans have become "totally changed to a conscious level of involvement in the struggle for [their] own mind liberation." (1988, p. 49) Perhaps Dr. Martin Luther King, the great civil rights activist and Nobel Peace Prize winner, would roll over in his grave if he knew blacks were deliberately 're-segregating' themselves, as he fought his entire adult life for the ideals and principles of 'integration.'

The idea, however, of a truly separate nation of blacks and whites is a notion that many blacks and whites in America would reject *out-right*, for many are opposed to the absolute separation of the races, and believe that the only way that we can survive as a sovereign and free nation is by *total* integration and unification—hence, a *multi-racial democracy*.

Finally, and even though fierce opponents, critics, and scholars such as professor Mary Lefkowitz, Pat Buchanan, George Will, and William Bennett, would refute the whole Afrocentric notion (Coughlin, 1996, pp. A6-A7), or black nationalist idea (or black frame of references) as being culturally biased and elitist. Afrocentrism, nonetheless, is now embraced by many black intellectuals and scholars—even laymen—as a serious academic discipline. And despite what many might think to the contrary—that is, of the futility and weakness of the Afrocentric philosophy—it is here to stay as a valid educational field or discipline, as blacks in America will always accept a sort of nationalistic identity or racial aesthetic. Ultimately, black studies, no doubt, will become a vital part of the core college curriculum in the near future, despite the noisy and vociferous opposition by conservative and even liberal opponents.

POLITICAL LIBERALISM

From the outset, it must be understood that American liberalism has been criticized "for having institutionalized pluralist competition at the expense of those unable to compete..." (Pfaff, 1969, p. 49). According to Francis Fukuyama (1993, p. 42), however, American political liberalism should be "defined simply as a rule of law that recognizes certain individual rights or freedoms from government control."

If we accept what Fukuyama says as correct, it raises a central question: Why, if there are supposedly no problems with our individual rights and freedoms, do many blacks and other minorities in America continue to suffer needlessly and not benefit fully from such constitutional or guaranteed freedoms? Furthermore, if "the liberal view of history...[asserts] that the plight of Blacks in America [has] been determined by [black] slavery and segregation..." (Zinn, 1990, p. 167), why can't African Americans transcend their difficult plight or predicament?

Such a provocative and controversial question is enough to launch many intense debates. However, one must understand that, since blacks are currently the largest minority in America, the principles of justice, liberty and 'equality of opportunity' are essential to their livelihood and survival. Moreover, the goal of eliminating all manner of discrimination should be the ultimate objective of any true democracy. However, "institutionalized access to the basic opportunities a society owes all of its citizens, are not (sic) always enforced...," (Raspberry, 1987, p. A-23) protected or provided.

Unfortunately, it seems that many black Americans have always been denied real access to many of these opportunities. For example, Professor James Harvey (1973, p. 3), in his path-breaking book, *Black Civil Rights During the Johnson Administration*, writes:

> Recognition by the federal government of the cruelly harsh conditions under which most black people have been forced to live has been slow in coming in this country. Yet, recognition at the federal level has been badly needed, since state and local governments have attempted little in improving the lot of blacks (and other minorities).

The above passage from Professor Harvey's book, written back in the 1970s, is important to note, because when one *critically* and *seriously* considers a liberal, he or she usually thinks of or envisions an individual who holds autonomy or hegemonic and equal political and cultural views that are quite opposite to those of conservatives, who "generally favor a more limited government role in regulating the economic market place" (Lasser, 1996, p. 163), and providing programs for the disadvantaged. This is especially true if the actions of (our) government do not benefit conservatives.

It must be clearly understood that liberals, on the other hand, "favor an active [and positive] government role in regulating economic activities, redistributing wealth, and expanding programs to help the poor and middle class" (Lasser, 1996, p. 163), primarily because no one *really* cares about the poor (or so it seems). This is especially important to understand when examining black aesthetics and multiculturalism in higher education—and in our society, for that matter. All liberal Americans must recognize that conservative Republicans would have us believe that the United States Education Department is not necessary, and therefore, it should be disbanded. However, we must also recognize that this vital governmental department essentially addresses many of our major multicultural/ educational concerns, as well as our pedagogical ideas and principles. What exactly, then, would the elimination of such a government bureaucracy solve? And what would be the cost benefits?

All in all, blacks, native Americans, Hispanics, and the truly downtrodden (or inclusively minorities) must have government intervention and assistance (especially in educational endeavors) if they are to be treated fairly or equally, and if we are to have a truly democratic and multi-racial society. This begs the question: Can the white majority do the right thing for minorities in this country? Indeed, how can all Americans achieve a middle-class life style without help or government intervention? Ultimately, I say, and perhaps Fukuyama would agree, that it is absolutely amazing that we live in a country where we all—at least—have the opportunity to knock down certain barriers to succeed in American society, and even to discuss these important racial and controversial issues. In the final analysis, it must be noted that there is no rational basis for *not* accepting Black Studies and Multiculturalism at all levels of the educational spectrum in our society. Learning about these matters, certainly, shows open-mindedness. As Professor Diane Ravitch (1990, p. 354) has cogently written:

> It has been important for blacks—and for other racial groups—to learn about the history of slavery and of the civil rights movement; it has been important for blacks to know that their ancestors actively resisted enslavement and actively pursued equality; and it has been important for blacks and others to learn about black men and women who fought courageously against racism and

who provide models of courage, persistence, and intellect. These are instances where the content of the curriculum reflects sound scholarship, and at the same time probably lessens racial prejudice and provides inspiration for those who are descendants of slaves.

In conclusion, we must understand that "separatist education [may] presents every bit the threat to national community that separatist politics and separatist *entitlements* do" (Wilkinson, 1997, p. 151). However, we must also ask: Do all Americans really care about minorities and black people, and how do these minorities feel exactly about being in a predominantly white society—which created separate societies and the distinct racist and educational systems we have in the United States in the first place? According to Robert Kuttner, "nearly every great social justice movement was initiated by radicals before it became safe for liberals. This includes the antislavery movement, women's [and blacks'] suffrage…modern feminism…[and] civil rights" (Kuttner, 2000, p. 4). But, as long as 'white supremacy' and racism exist, there will always be a problem with radical minorities not conforming to the wishes—or even the educational and societal goals—of the dominant group.

REFERENCES

Asante, Molefi K. 1988. *Afrocentricity*. Trenton, New Jersey: Africa World Press, Inc.

Bennett, W. J. 1988. *American Education: Making It Work: A Report to the President and the American People*. Washington, D.C.: U.S. Department of Education.

Boynton, Robert S. 1995, March. "The New Intellectuals." *The Atlantic Monthly*.

Budiansky, Stephen. 1993, February 1. "Pioneering Integration: When the Army Took the Lead." *U.S. News and World Report*.

Burns, James M., *et. al.* 1995. *Government By the People*. National Version, 16th edition. Englewood Cliffs, New Jersey: Prentice Hall.

Ceaser, James W. 1990. *Liberal Democracy and Political Science*. Baltimore, Maryland. Johns Hopkins University Press.

Coughlin, Ellen K. 1996, February 16. "Not Out of Africa." *The Chronicle of Higher Education*.

Fukuyama, Francis. 1993. *The End of History and the Last Man*. New York: Avon.

Fulwood, Sam III. 1995, November 10. "Frustrated Blacks Turning Away From White Society." *Las Vegas Review Journal*.

Harvey, James C. 1973. *Black Civil Rights During the Johnson Administration*. Jackson, Mississippi: University and College Press of Mississippi.

Kuttner, Robert. 2000. "Why Liberals Need Radicals." *The American Prospect*.

Lasser, William. 1996. *American Politics*. Lexington, Massachusetts: D.C. Heath and Company.

Pfaff, William. 1969, October. "The Decline of Liberal Politics." *Commentary*. Vol. 48, No. 4.

Raspberry, William. 1987, February 25. "The Civil Rights Movement Is Over." *The Washington Post*.

Ravitch, Diane. 1990. "Multiculturalism: E. Pluribus Plures." *American Scholar*.

Sitkoff, Harvard. 1971, November. "Harry Truman and the Election of 1948: The Coming of Age of Civil Rights in American Politics." *The Journal of Southern History*. Vol. 37.

Wilkinson, J. Harvie III. 1997. *One Nation Indivisible: How Ethnic Separatism Threatens America*. reading, Massachusetts: Addison-Wesley Publishing Company, Inc.

Williams, Chancellor. 1987. *The Destruction of Black Civilization: Great Issues of A Race From 4500 B.C. To 2000 A.D.* Chicago, Illinois: Third World Press;

Zinn, Howard. 1990. *The Politics of History*. 2nd edition. Urbana and Chicago: University of Illinois Press.

The Legacy of African American Leadership in the Present and for the Future: On Black Community

INTRODUCTION

In order to understand Black leadership in the United States—today and for the future—it is absolutely necessary to know *something* first about the development of Black American history and culture and the relationship between white culture and white civilizations. According to Professor Anthony Walton:

The history of African-Americans during the past 400 years is traditionally narrated as an ongoing struggle against oppression and indifference on the part of the American mainstream, a struggle charted as an upward arc progressing toward ever more justice and opportunity. (1999, p. 16)

This description is accurate, but there is another way of interpreting and explaining black, diasporic history. For example, America has been a place where African Americans have been relegated to the political and economic fringes. Blacks have even been described by racists as being lower than many animal species. Therefore, many blacks are outside the American mainstream. Nonetheless, and to be sure, "black leadership and politics represent a quest for effective political power" (Prestage, 1968, p. 462).

Equally important, "there are many profound problems facing black America today" (1990, p. 20), as pointed out by Shelby Steele, former professor of English at San Jose State University and Research Fellow at the Hoover Institution, such as:

> a swelling black underclass; a black middle class that declined slightly in size during the Eighties; a declining number of black college students; an epidemic of teenage pregnancy, drug use, and gang violence; continuing chronic unemployment; astoundingly high school dropout rates; an increasing number of single-parent families; a disproportionately high infant mortality rate; and so on. (Steele, 1990, p. 20)

If these problems are so acute and epidemic, we must ask: How can African American leaders play a part in rectifying these issues in the continuing struggle against oppression? This is the dilemma faced today by many so-called leaders who must try to balance the demands of minorities, the poor and disadvantaged, and white philanthropists.

Moreover, who's running the show, so to speak, in the black community today? What black leader holds our imagination, provokes all of us toward achieving higher goals and opportunities, and provides a vision for the future? Furthermore, what black personality has what it takes to lead? Where are all of the black leaders today? Where have they gone? Indeed, who is the 'racial broker' in mainstream American politics? Or who is the main black power broker for the black community? Isn't there one leader who can step forward and speak for all of the black population in America—some thirty-five million strong?

It is as if we have unconsciously lost *something* in the United States today. But one must clearly understand that Black America, as a whole, has *never* known *exactly* what they have wanted in terms of a leader. Professor Henry Louis Gates, Jr., Chairman of the African American Studies Program of Harvard University, "has publicly criticized the notion that there are leaders who are singular representative of the race" (Reed, 1995, p. 36).

Ultimately, the overwhelming majority of black Americans today remain *conscious* only of what black leaders *have not* done for America's dispossessed, not what they have accomplished. Unfortunately, our embattled black leaders today have also basically shied away from recognizing the status of all blacks in every walk-of-life—or other unfortunate classes of black people—especially in representing the extremely poor. The emphasis seem to be on not losing any more ground in terms of civil rights and equality of opportunity in almost all areas of American life. In fact, "most black leaders still look expectantly to intervention by the federal government as the principal means of improving the [political and] economic status of the black community"

(Brimmer, 1985, p. 39). But this is a pipe dream if African Americans think the government's help will happen anytime soon or in the distant future.

THE IDEOLOGICAL DEBATE

According to black political scientist at Stanford University, Lucius Barker, "There are two types of [black] leaders: those who emerge from the pack and those who stand away from the pack and get people to follow" (Lang, 1991, p. A10). Referring to the traditional black leader, in the mold of W.E.B. DuBois, Marcus Garvey, Shirley Chisholm, or Barbara Jordan, Professor Barker goes on to state that, "Most of the black leaders on the political scene today have emerged from the pack and [basically], reflect the political views of the vast majority of black people" (Lang, 1991, p. A10)

However, we must also consider the so-called black conservative leader, whose "authenticity is conferred [mostly] by white opinion makers" (Reed, 1995, p. 34). Depending on your point of view, these black conservative leaders do not speak for the black community either, as we will discuss later in this chapter. And sadly, as Barker has explained:

> Those in the forefront of the black conservative trend are those who have separated themselves from baseline politics of the black community and have come to prominence in national politics without the support of black constituents. (Lang, 1991, p. A10)

In recent year, moreover, black leaders, of any ilk, have not attracted a lot of support and attention. However, there has been notable exceptions, such as Louis Farrakhan. Farrakhan, of course, can predictably rouse a crowd of African Americans in almost any forum, but he does not enjoy the broad support in the political mainstream necessary to say he leads all black people. Indeed, one might also ask: Did the late Khallid Muhammad, organizer of the 1998 Million Youth March in New York City and once Farrakhan's flamboyant and incendiary militant defense minister, speak for the black community in America? Perhaps not. Nevertheless, the controversial leader and fiery public speaker of *The Final Call to the Nation of Islam*, Farrakhan, has preached "a vision of political separatism, and a program of moral rearmament, "self-help," business development and an idiosyncratic brand of Islamic religion" (Reed, 1991, p. 51)

It is also worth noting that Farrakhan was once Elijah Muhammad's national representative of the Nation of Islam. But after Elijah Muhammad's death and when his son and successor, Wallace, announced that White Americans could join the organization, Farrakhan separated from the main, black Islamic group. Farrakhan was perhaps outraged by this unacceptable and untenable development. Therefore, he overwhelmingly rejected the Nation of Islam created by Elijah Muhammad and started his own more radical splinter organization. Farrakhan continues to work reportedly "for black separatism, which he feels can best be advanced by strengthening the economic power of the black community" (Smith, 1994, p. 55); however, most black Americans do not share or embrace his philosophy. According to director of the Institute for Research in African-American Studies at Columbia University and Professor of History, Manning Marable:

> Today many of the same economic ideas are being championed by two seemingly very different black leaders: Colin Powell and Louis Farrakhan. Both men would favor blacks becoming "less reliant" on government programs; both support efforts at black entrepreneurship; both probably believe that the black middle class has the unique responsibility to uplift the rest of the black community. Although one leader is the darling of moderate Republicanism and white suburbia and the other has his core constituency in the black inner cities, that does not alter the similarities of their economic argument. (1999, p. 184)

However, Farrakhan's message has not reached all of America's black masses and probably never will. Many white Americans, of course, think Farrakhan is a militant and false prophet, as well as anti-Jewish. Nonetheless, his distinctive voice has been a soothing catharsis for many African Americans, and he has emerged, albeit reluctantly, as a national political figure. This was quite evident during his successful organization and conduct of the Million Man March in Washington, D.C. in 1995. Farrakhan's emotional speeches and divisive rhetoric, unfortunately, have alienated many white and black Americans who see him, perhaps, as a leader who could have made a difference in race-relations and maybe their own lives. Farrakhan, of course, got to this point through a mixture of guile, background, charisma, and character. And according to political journalist and writer, Adolph Reed:

> Farrakhan stands out because he has been cast in our public theater—like Qaddafi and Noriega, both of whom he has defended—as a figure of almost…demonic proportions. He has become uniquely notorious because his inflammatory nationalist persona has helped to center public discussion of Afro American politics on the only issue (except affirmative action, of course) about which most whites ever show much concern: What do blacks think of whites? (Rueter, 1995, p. 84)

As the above passage indicates, Farrakhan (as long as he lives) will continue to play a significant role in our political system in the near future. But on the other side of the black leadership spectrum, we must seriously reflect on the outspoken and pragmatic leader of the civil rights struggle, the Reverend Jesse Jackson.

As an influential and rousing Baptist preacher, Democratic Presidential candidate in 1984 and 1988; head of Operation Breadbasket of the Southern Christian Leadership Conference (SCLC), and chairman of PUSH and the Rainbow Coalition, the enigmatic Jackson has not only made his considerable mark on American public life, but he has also become a public celebrity as the host of his own TV program, called Both Sides with Jesse Jackson.

One has to wonder, however, if Jackson thought Dr. King's shoes were very big to fill and that he would probably *always* be following in them. Jackson has admitted that he benefited from his involvement with Dr. King and the privileges and recognition that went with his apparent take-over of the reign or civil rights movement after Dr. King's death, but Jackson has made his own way. For example, Jackson absolutely galvanized the black community when he first ran for president. And after both of his runs for president in 1984 and 1988, he became a seasoned politician. Jackson, of course, was pragmatic enough to know, however, that basing a presidential campaign on the rights of blacks in the United States would not get him very far. Therefore, Jackson had to change strategies, to be more realistic, especially in getting whites to vote for him, which they did in great numbers. And as journalist Debbie Howlett has ventured, Jackson "remains a player in presidential politics. Though President Clinton [was] popular among African-Americans, Jackson is still described as the president of black America" (Howlett, 1996, p. 6A), despite his recent infidelity problems.

Former President Ronald Reagan was once quoted as saying, "You can't argue with success," about Jackson's negotiations with Syrian leader Hafez Assad and the successful release of a black Navy pilot shot down in the Middle East over Lebanon, as well as his success in negotiating with former Yugoslav President Slobodan Milosevic in the releases of three American detainees: Army specialist Steven Gonzales and Staff Sergeants Andrew Ramirez and Christopher J. Stone. Jackson has also be credited with brokering "a cease-fire in Sierra Leone" (Howlett, 1996, p. 6A).

In this sense, Jesse Jackson does not limit his concerns to the black community, though he remains influential, regardless of the fact that many African Americans do not believe he speaks for them, either. Nonetheless, as Howlett has written, "no one seems inclined to publicly assail Jackson at this point. By sitting on the presidential sidelines and succeeding in his Yugoslavia trip, Jackson...silenced all but the die-hard critics" (Howlett, 1996, p. 6A).

Additionally, and equally important, we must concern ourselves with the new leaders of the NAACP, Kweisi Mfume, who is the current president and CEO of the organization, and the veteran civil rights activist and NAACP Board Chairman, Julian Bond. It should be noted that Mfume was once touted as being a viable candidate for the mayor of Baltimore, Maryland. However, he declined to run. After serving as the president of the Congressional Black Caucus for several years in the House of Representatives, Mfume took over the oldest civil rights organization—with approximately 350,000 members or more, and 2,200 local branches and 64 policy-setting national board members—in 1997.

Mfume, of course, brought his hard-driving leadership and agility to the NAACP that made him famous and a successful Congressman from Maryland. And after some misgivings within the ranks of the grand old civil rights organization in the United States, he was confirmed as the group's modern-day leader. Accustomed to a less formal leadership style, Mfume is now in the political limelight of leadership by virtue of his coveted position, emerging mightily from the pipeline or pack of would-be black leaders of the NAACP organization.

On the other hand, the well-known Julian Bond, one of the founders of the Student Nonviolent Coordinating Committee (SNCC), has been a part of the civil rights battle for years. He has also been an elected state representative in Georgia and served as the leader of the local NAACP chapter in Atlanta. Bond is also one of the co-founders of the Southern Poverty Law Center, the organization that monitors and investigates hate groups in America. The charming and debonair Mr. Bond is now a college professor at American University in Washington, D.C., and a TV personality.

An eloquent spokesman, Julian Bond has become almost a mythic or legendary figure in the cause for social and economic justice for African Americans, and this has enhanced the credibility and membership rolls of the NAACP in recent years. Bond has outlined an energetic campaign for the largest civil rights group, and he sees the main mission of the NAACP as "fighting white supremacy to death" (Thomas, 1999, p. 8B).

The dynamic black duo—Mfume and Bond—are still trying to sort out how to strengthen the NAACP membership base and lead under difficult circumstances, as well as recover from the false start of the disgraced Dr. Benjamin Chavis, who was accused of using NAACP funds for his own personal use. In essence, these two elected NAACP leaders (Bond and Mfume) represent a substantial black constituency. But are *they* truly representative of all American blacks?

In both cases, we must not underrate Bond and Mfume's significance, because unfortunately, such leadership has been in relatively short supply lately. In other words, these traditional leaders are few and far between. Which begs the following questions: What are the motives or motivation of black leaders today? And who will be the new leaders of the future? And ultimately, what will these leaders be able to do for us and what can black Americans do for them?

All of these questions are valid and especially important to understand, because even now "the traditional leadership of the American Negro community—a leadership which has been largely middle class in origin and orientation—is in danger of losing its claim to speak for the masses of Negroes" (Mayfield, 1961, p. 297).

In a sense, Journalist Julian Mayfield's remarkable prediction back in 1961 has come true, as we can say that the middle-class (or bourgeois) black leaders *have* lost their voice throughout America. And if we are to understand the dangers of their losing their rightful claim to speak for African Americans, or their demise, we must also be cognizant of this middle-class leadership, and one leader in particular—Dr. Martin Luther King, Jr.

Dr. King, of course, helped shaped the way in which we look at race and bigotry in this country, and for nearly the entire period of his adult life, he seriously challenged the actions of the traditional, radical, and so-called Black leaders.

Dr. King also saw the expansion of the techniques of non-violence and civil disobedience, as espoused by Mahatma Gandhi of India, and he helped redefine the civil rights movement by his powerful message, his oratory skills, and his condemnation of racial intolerance and injustice.

Dr. King is also important as a symbolic reminder of where we have been and where we are going as a nation in terms of race relations. Indeed, Dr. King has become the very embodiment of the American civil rights movement.

This is important to note, because unfortunately, many of our so-called leaders today—and this includes the best and brightest of the young, black, conservative Turks—"are [sadly] interested primarily in their own self-promotion and financial gain, rather than in whether or not Black people will suffer" (Smiley, 1996, p. 37).

And then we must bear in mind the long *apprenticeship* in the black nationalist tradition and black radical movement itself—that is, of older, and now almost voiceless, black revolutionary leaders, like Amiri Baraka, or even the late James Baldwin, who was also one of our foremost black writers. Indeed, such intense preparation by such leaders did not make truly a black national leader. Conservative scholar and black economist Thomas Sowell has written:

> In many cases, their very "leadership" consist[ed] not of their having been selected by blacks but of being regarded by the white news media, white philanthropy and white politicians as "spokesmen" for the black masses. Much of the black leadership is not in the business of leading blacks but of extracting what they can from whites, and their strategies and rhetoric reflect that orientation. (Sowell, 1991)

Nonetheless, the late Malcolm X proved just the opposite of Sowell's contentious statement, because he had the power and ability not only to influence people, without the help of white people, but to quickly take over the national scene by manipulating and disturbing his followers and mostly black audiences—to a certain degree—to action, as he spoke to us in those little dark, secret places inside each and everyone of us.

And *no one* reached the mood and psyche wounds of blacks better than Malcolm X. In fact, Malcolm X, along with Dr. Martin Luther King, Jr., was one of the best known black advocates for *true* equality, freedom, and first-class citizenship for African Americans. But Malcolm X believed blacks should take their rights by any means necessary. Now, what black leader can say that today, or claim the mantle of leadership for the future?

Through considerable soul searching, Malcolm X later changed his militant "black power" stance and his political philosophy, after visiting Mecca and the Middle East and getting a true taste or glimpse of what it really meant to be a Muslim. Moreover, Malcolm X began to moderate his hostile views of white Americans after forming the Organization of Afro-American Unity. But for this bold and unprecedented move, Malcolm X paid with his life, as he was assassinated by opponents, those disenchanted, disgruntled, and dissident blacks who thought Malcolm X had sold out.

In a different vein from Malcolm X, Dr. Martin Luther King, Jr., and the others I have already mentioned in this chapter, no one today seems to be *really* jockeying to be heard, or maneuvering to the forefront to fight only for the rights of minorities in this country. In other words, you don't exactly see *anyone* bursting across the scene of our American landscape to take charge— like a benign Al Sharpton—to speak for us all, including the black poor. Even more important, a legacy of bad feelings, scapegoating, and mean-spiritness exist among whites in America. And the debate between black liberals and conservatives has not made things better or easier for the on-going struggle for African Americans, either.

Toward this end, and sparked at least in part by the expectation of the control of the black intellectual leadership, has been the debate between black conservatives and black liberals. Black conservative leaders, according to the nationally known black television and radio commentator, Tavis Smiley, are similar to those Africans who "aided slave traders in the search and capture of other Africans—wittingly or otherwise…" (Smiley, 1996, p. 36). Smiley writes:

> Black conservatives [like Ward Connerly of California and Supreme Court Judge Clarence Thomas] have aided and abetted efforts to roll-back many of the hard-won social, economic, and political gains among the African American community over the past forty years. (Smiley, 1996, p. 36)

Generally speaking, black conservative leaders believe that there is more than one side to the question of race in America. However, as Smiley goes on to write scathingly, "Black conservative [leaders] have allowed themselves to be used to carry out the dirty work of closed-minded people who do not have the interests of African Americans and poor people at heart. Worse, they lend *credibility* to views that are misguided and often racist" (1996, p. 36).

In this sense, I firmly believe that the vast majority of the black community will *never* follow (totally) the emerging black conservative leaders, because most "have few direct ties to or roots in the black community or black institutions such as churches, fraternities, professional groups or civil rights organizations" (Lang, 1991, p. A18).

However, black conservatives like the first modern black conservative member of Congress, Gary Franks, and former Congressman and Republican Conference Chairman, J.C. Watts, Jr. defy convention and the traditional Republican label. Watts, for example, is a Baptist minister at the Bethlehem Baptish Church in Lawton, Oklahoma, with extremely long ties to that community. Many black conservatives and whites, moreover, still see Watts as a rising star and major leader of the Republican Party. (Baldauf, 1999, p. 1) But it remains to be seen if Watts's conservative and bitter *voice* can reach a broader black audience in the United States, especially since he recently resigned from Congress. Or, to put it another way, such black conservatives, like J.C. Watts, Jr., are "without any rank and file following, men who speak *for* the Negro [or Black] community, but who rarely speak to it, men who simply assume that some massive vote of confidence has been awarded them" (Walzer,

1960, p. 237). Nothing can be further from the truth, however. Because *they* do not speak for 'black America,' either.

CONCLUSIONS

It should also be said that black conservative leaders do not say anything positive about African Americans, nor have they said "anything remotely *challenging* to White America" (Smiley, 1996, p. 37). Indeed, no black conservative leader has recently spoken out on pressing issues of immediate concern to the black community in a positive way.

Fortunately, as far as black liberals are concerned, who are arguably *more* representative of blacks in America, it seems they (our liberal leaders) today are the academic "superstars," or they are from the academic community. In fact, many black celebrity scholars, like Ron Karenga and Molefi Asante, "have used their prestigious university positions to extend their influence beyond the academy" (Boynton, 1995, p. 56). We can also look at moderate black academics, such as Henry Louis Gates, a MacArthur Genius Award winner, the chair of the Afro-American Studies Department at Harvard, and a recent recipient of the Presidential Medal of Freedom, the nation's highest civilian honor. In addition, he is a National Book award winner in 1988 for his path-breaking book, *The Signifying Monkey*.

Political journalist Robert S. Boynton supports the contention of the black academic specialists becoming today's black leaders when he wrote:

> Outstanding [black] students who ten years before would most likely have become political activists instead pursued academic careers. As a result, many developed an intellectual style with a decidedly activist edge, in the university but not completely of it, theirs is scholarship with a social purpose. (1995, p. 64)

Former black student leaders and "black power" activists, like Bell Hooks and Cornel West, for example, are now university professors of some noteworthiness at major white educational institutions. Consider the prominent educator and lecturer, Dr. Cornel West, who has become a highly regarded and respected writer and post-modern intellectual. Indeed, his best-selling and celebrated book, *Race Matters* has become a modern classic. Boynton, furthermore, writes that, "Black thinkers who want to make changes in the wider public-intellectual culture have a better chance working from within the university than outside it" (1995, p. 65).

However, the idiosyncratic West, according to Adolph Reed, "has postured as a link to black activist authenticity, holding an honorary leadership position in the Democratic Socialists of America and referring frequently to associations with supposed grassroots leaders and organizations" (1995, p. 35). We must also consider the community and civil rights activists who are now participating in our government by becoming elected officials, like Bobby Rush, the former Black Panther and Congressman, who lost a bitter mayoral election against Richard Daley in Chicago. Rush still serves in the House of Representatives today.

But besides the action of these liberal politicians or the intellectual contributions of academic upstarts, what have they done exactly for the average black, working-class American? Unfortunately, we can perhaps conclude that they haven't actually put food in the mouths of many poor black people or African Americans. In fairness to the black conservative leadership, moreover, and even though most liberal black leaders incorporate a heavy *dose* of self-help themes, the majority of them *advocate* a stronger government role, such as affirmative action programs, to redress past discrimination. (Lang, 1991, p. A10)

This, of course, is not the only answer. And one thing is clear: after the debate over whether black conservatives or black liberals have more influence as leaders, it is *unlikely* that any one black person will emerge or present himself or herself as the *new* or definitive voice for African Americans in the near future. Or perhaps this is an unfair assessment.

But why wouldn't or would black people be interested in a new, freshly-minted black leader coming forward from the 'ashes of despair' to speak for all African Americans? This question, of course, is significant. Therefore, whoever steps forward as a black leader must be intelligent, resolute, and able to touch the black world—or all aspects of the black diasporic community—serving as a strong role model especially to uplift the disillusioned black youth in this nation. In the final analysis, the black leaders of tomorrow must be farsighted enough to strike a balance with critics, fierce opponents, and black conservatives, as well as to take advantage of the opportunities made available by any source or means available.

Furthermore, this new black leader must be held accountable for his or her leadership and actions. The new black leader must also have a positive message, wielding a positive influence for the black masses, while noting the incredible diversity within the black community—and not wanting to control *everything*, or centralize and approve everything in advance that concerns African Americans. In other words, power must be shared. The new leader should certainly know these things in order to advance his activities and agenda, because in a very real way, we find our condition unchanged in the United States, "despite some impressive increases in the number of black people holding public office, despite our ability now to sit and eat and ride and vote and go to school in places which used to bar black faces..." (Bond, 1990, pp. 275-276).

Further, the simmering conflict or ideological battles taking place among black intellectuals and various black groups in the United States must stop immediately—that is, if we are to survive as a multi-racial democracy, and as a people. Finally, the future black leader must follow through on *any* promises he or she may make to the black masses, if conceivably possible—or not make the promises in the first place.

That means that, all things being equal, the black leaders of the future must focus and coordinate the communications and efforts of other civil rights organizations and black activist groups—to make sure they are over-whelmingly together on the many important issues that may or may not affect the lives of all Americans, most especially blacks who live within the confines of the United States.

But no matter what kind of leader presents himself or herself on the political landscape or challenging horizon, we must work steadily to bridge the gap that exists among all Americans. In the ultimate analysis, the black leader of tomorrow must lead decisively for the greater good of African Americans, the black community, and all Americans—or get out of the way.

REFERENCES

Baldauf, Scott. 1999, March 9. "J.C. Watts, Jr.: For Republicans, A Different Leader." *The Christian Science Monitor.*

Bond, Julian. 1990. "Where We've Been, Where We're Going: A Vision of Racial Justice in the 1990's." *Harvard Civil Rights—Civil Liberties Law Review.* Vol. 25.

Boynton, Robert S. 1995, March. "The New Intellectuals." *The Atlantic Monthly.*

Brimmer, Andrew. 1985, November. "The Future of Blacks in the Public Sector." *Black Enterprise.*

Howlett, Debbie. 1999, August 6. "Jackson finds new passion, new popularity." *USA Today.*

Lang, Perry. 1991, July 6. "Black Conservatives in Spotlight." *San Francisco Chronicle.*

Mayfield, Julian. 1961, April. "Challenge to Negro Leadership: The Case of Robert Williams." *Commentary.* No. 3.

Prestage, Jewell L. 1968, December. "Black Politics and the Kerner Report Concerns and Direction." *Social Science Quarterly.* Vol. 49.

Reed, Adolph. 1995, April 11. "The Current Crisis of the Black Intellectual." *Village Voice.* 1991, January 21. "False Prophet: The Rise of Louis Farrakhan." *The Nation.*

Smiley, Tavis. 1996. *Hard Left: Straight Talk about the Wrongs of the Rights.* New York: Anchor Books, Doubleday.

Smith, Sande. 1994. editor. *Who's Who in African-American History.* New York: Smith-Mark Publisher, Inc.

Sowell, Thomas. 1990, October 29. "Led and Misled." *The New York Times.*

Steel, Shelby. 1990, May. "Ghettoized By Black Unity." *Harper's Magazine.*

Thomas, Cal. 1999, February 23. "New slave on a new government plantation." *Las Vegas Review-Journal.*

Walton, Anthony. 1999, January. "Technology Versus African-Americans." *The Atlantic Monthly.* Vol. 283, No. 1.

Walzer, Michael. 1960, Summer. "The Politics of the New Negro." *Dissent.*

African Dreams:
On Keith B. Richburg's
Out of America

Hong Kong bureau chief for *The Washington Post*, Keith B. Richburg wrote an intriguing, important, and controversial book in 1997, whose provocative title *Out of America: A Black Man Confronts Africa* reminds all displaced Africans or blacks in the Diaspora that not all blacks in the Americas are out of Africa.

As a black American reporter, raised in a poor Detroit ghetto, who spent three appalling (to his particular frame of mind) years in Africa, Richburg was well placed to provide all Americans with evidence of "irrefutable truths," as well as disillusioning facts about the senseless brutality, squalor, viciousness, and barbarism in several African states he visited in the heart of the so-called Dark Continent.

Furthermore, as a correspondent for the *Washington Post* from 1991 to 1994, Richburg had direct responsibility for reporting about the butchery and human suffering, the indiscriminate killings in Rwanda, Nairobi, Sierra Leone, and outright slavery in Somalia and other dangerous places he magnificently writes about, without which we could not have known the *intimate* and shocking details of the area at the time. In his own exciting and engaging words, Richburg believed that it was up to him "to expose the suffering, to make the world pay attention." Indeed, his bitter life in Africa seemed absolutely surreal and perplexing because of the horrible and sickening atrocities that occurred and he had the misfortune to witness first hand in the home of his ancestors.

Agreed: some of the African countries Richburg visited were the cause of their own miserable predicaments—that is, the rampant coups d'etat, the campaigns of ethnic cleansing and genocide, anti-democratic repression, as well as the corruption of despotic African leaders and tyrants (or African dictators in charge); and the age-old problem of denials of human rights, as well as suppression of most freedoms—thus the crushing of individual thought and strong (African) nationhood.

Richburg finally understood that he, as well as most black Americans could never go home to the mother-land without risking personal peril or even death. Richburg writes of a particularly disturbing incident in Somalia where he was almost murdered by Somali gunmen or thugs with AK 47 assault rifles, who thought he was Somali. "All because I was a black man in the wrong place, a black man in Africa," (1997, p. 88) Richburg sadly writes. Similarly, as veteran newspaper columnist and essayist Jim Sleeper points out:

> While black American pilgrims to Africa were newly preoccupied with the significance of being "black," they found that designation has no significance in most of Africa. There, the same skin color encompasses multitudes of cultural and tribal differences and is no more useful a moral or political lens than is "white" in the Balkans or, for that matter, in Scandinavia. Many Africans, recognizing their black visitors immediately as Americans, treated them as aliens having nothing in common with Africans who hadn't studied here [in the United States] or followed America culture. (Sleeper, 1997, p. 106)

Truth to tell, the years that it took Richburg to finally piece together and write the book allowed him to reflect thoughtfully, and do some soul-searching on his adventures or misadventures in Africa. Richburg's story is one that had to be told (again) and was very much reminiscent of screenwriter and black journalist Eddy L. Harris's popular 1992 book, *Native Stranger: A Black American's Journey into the Heart of Africa*, where he too became disillusioned with a distant place they both thought would embrace and welcome them as long lost brothers or relatives; a place they could identify with, be enamored with and love. But they both were sadly mistaken. In addition to sharing structure and a rousing tale of Africa, both *Out of America* and *Native Strangers* are interesting African travel stories.

The similarities, moreover, are striking and obvious and cannot be ignored: Blacks in America are not 'native-born' Africans, nor does the African continent have much to do with American blacks living in the Disapora (e.g., Belize, Virgin Islands, or Brazil), which descendants of slaves can call, if you will, home. In other words, blacks can romanticize about Africa as being a place where they can one day return to as their ancestral homeland in glorious triumph, but it exists only in their collective hopes and dreams. More specifically, Africans in Africa do not necessarily see blacks in America as brothers. This is a sad commentary, of course, and is one of Africa's strangest and confusing paradoxes.

Which is to say, black Americans' ethnic links to Africa have done little to protect those would be returnees from exclusion, isolation, and even harassment from native born Africans. These things, unfortunately, keep the blacks in the Diaspora who would like to live (somewhere) in Africa in this uncomfortable paradox of which we speak—torn between two worlds—which essentially means blacks must immigrate to a mean-spirited African country, regardless of the known dangers, or remain in their many adopted lands throughout the world.

Both densely layered works, *Out of America* and *Native Strangers* provide provocative analyses of Africa that shed considerable light on what actually goes on in several of these authoritarian African nations. For example, they both warn of the dire consequences of being poor, wretched (black) and powerless, because as in most places in the world, such people have no real voice.

Richburg's reflections do not present a lot of solutions, however, and may not sit well with many Pan-nationalists or Afrocentrists, as the book has prompted heated debates among black scholars for its critical and scathing account of African leaders and even some American black leaders, like Jesse Jackson and Coretta Scott King, who visited and unfortunately embraced some of these ruthless and tyrannical black strongmen, especially as he observed them during his African journey. Richburg's book, however, is far more than just an indictment of African and African American leaders.

It would be also folly not taking into account the many failed and ruined economies in many African states, as they are *rife* with corruption, especially after European colonialism. Some scholars even believe that many African countries are far worse off today than under white colonialism. Richburg's brief economic analysis of the past and present governmental policies of these countries is particularly sound. African stability, one learns, must extend (beyond respective borders), to include political, physical and economic security.

There are a number of imponderables in assessing whether African countries can survive in a growing cosmopolitan world. It is likely that many will be subject to the threat of those black military leaders or cutthroats, who would be kings or notable heads of state. Therefore, perhaps the only way many African states can secure peace and freedom, and a semblance of normalcy, is to ensure that they remain (absolutely) democratic with competent, honest black leaders who are beyond reproach, if possible, with active constitutions that stipulate civilian control over the various militaries. Otherwise, war between separate African nations, and from within, will continue to occur in many different ways. Professor George B.N. Ayittey in his 1992 book, *Africa Betrayed*, accurately asserts:

> When will African dictators be held accountable for their misdeeds? Holding these dictators to account is understandably difficult and dangerous in Africa. But "well-meaning" Westerners compound the problem by offering nonsensical excuses for the egregious actions of these tyrant. Past colonial iniquities or "an unfair trading" system gives no African leader the license to terrorize his people.

It may be cogently argued that it is not the responsibility of the West to guide Africa's destiny or police its affairs. Nor does the West have any moral right to meddle in the internal affairs of sovereign African nations. But the West cannot seek to defend human rights in some parts of the world and neglect them in Africa. (p. xvii)

So, should the West then not meddle anywhere? Moreover, can African states carry the burden that peace and freedom require or demand? Readers of Richburg's book should note the terrible consequences of being under tyrannical and brutal black rule. However, Africans, especially in South Africa, are making historical changes in Africa today for the inclusion of everyone. In this remarkable sense, there is, of course, another view and lighter side of Africa. But Richburg asks:

> How can anyone talk about democracy and the rule of law in places [in Africa] where paramilitary security forces firebomb the offices of opposition newspapers? Where entire villages get burned down and thousands of people made homeless because of competing political loyalties? Where whole chunks of countries are under the sway of armed guerrillas? And where traditional belief runs so deep that a politician can be arrested and charged with casting magic spells over poor villagers to force them to vote for him. (1997, pp. 226-227)

Some black American readers, moreover, may be disappointed if they hope to find confirmation of the "Mother Africa" notion, and others might even say that Richburg exaggerates the problems Africa face today. Nonetheless, *Not Out of America* is a lively, well-written account of his newspaper's assignments to the African bureau. Richburg is straight forward as he tried to portray accurately what is currently taking place on the African continent. He also succeeds admirably in exploring and relating not only his cultural "roots" or African *lineage*, but also the black aesthetics, historical and political *exigencies* that confronts Africa.

Even more important, it seems a long way off that African Americans can become a part of a United Africa, especially with the African AIDs epidemic, famine, starvation, black slavery in Sudan and elsewhere, wanton destruction and other hostilities continuing in many Africa countries. Moreover, Richburg deplores the political, economic, and social forces that are tearing the continent apart. Finally, at the end of his gruesome assignment, Richburg wrote, reflecting on how he felt while in Africa:

> I am a stranger here, adrift I look like them [black Africans], I can even alter my clothes a bit to appear less "Western," but I cannot understand what it is like to be one of them. True, my ancestors came from this place, and these are my distant cousins. But a chasm has opened up, a chasm of four hundred years and ten thousand miles. Nothing in my own past, nothing in my upbringing, has instilled in me my sense of what it must be like to be an African.... There is more, something far deeper, something that I am ashamed to admit: I am terrified of Africa. I don't want to be from this place.... I am quietly celebrating the passage of my ancestor who made it out. (1997, p. 233)

REFERENCES

Avittey, George B.N. 1992. *Africa Betrayed.* New York: St. Martin's Press.

Harris, Eddy L. 1992. *Native Stranger: A Black American's Journey into the Heart of Africa.* New York: Simon & Schuster.

Richburg, Keith B. 1997. *Out of America: A Black Man Confronts Africa.* New York: Basic Books.

Sleeper, Jim. 1997. *Liberal Racism.* New York: Viking.

The Life and Loves of Mr. Jiveass Nigger and How to Make Love to a Negro: Aesthetics, Sexual Politics, Racial Protest, and the Emergence of Risqué Black Literature

A sharp distinction must be made perhaps before saying that Dany Laferriere's farcical novel, *How to Make Love to a Negro* (1987) was shaped or inspired by Cecil Brown's "wildly comic satire of sex and race among black American Expatriates in Europe" (Early xii), *The Life and Loves of Mr. Jiveass Nigger* (1960), even though there are striking and readily recognized similarities in both of these unique books.

The difference may be illustrated by comparing Brown's description of a certain passage of introspection to Laferriere's hilarious account of blacks in Quebec, Canada, which are quite similar or analogous in the message they try to convey, but utterly different in tone, time periods, style or construction, perspective and composition. First, Brown writes:

> He was Mr. Jiveass Nigger himself, and knew that there was nothing under the sun that was really phony if it was functional.... But cats like Jero didn't relate to that. They related to Bigger Thomas. Yes, Bigger, who went through

life living masochistic nightmares, who in reality was a substitute for some psychic guilt…and thus spent their lives huddling like wet dogs around the fire and not having enough guts to go out there and see just what it is that's making that noise, yes all those stupid ass Biggers who think violence is sex, who don't have enough cool to seduce a "white" woman but who end up *stealing* a kiss from a "white" girl when he should have fucked her, fucked her so good she would have gotten a glimpse into the immortal soul of the universe and come away from it all a changed woman, fucked her so beautifully that she would come away feeling he was a man, that his fucking (his humanity) had brought out that core of goodness which is in the worst of thieves, that she would come away feeling he was a man, and not a nigger or an animal or an ex-gorilla or something (30-31).

Then Laferriere:

Things are going terribly wrong these days for the conscientious, professional black pick-up artist. The black period is over, has-been, kaput, finito, whited out. Nigger go home. *Va-t-en, Negro.* The Black Bottom's off the Top 20. *Hasta la vista, Negro.* Last call, colored man. Go back to the bush, man. Do yourself a hara-kiri you-know-where. Look, Mamma, says the Young White Girl, look at the Cut Negro. A good Negro, her father answers, is a Negro with no balls. In a nutshell, that's the situation in the 1980s, a dark day for Negro Civilization. On the stock market of the Western World, ebony has taken another spectacular fall. If only the Negro ejaculated oil. Black gold. O sadness, the Negro's sperm is ivory (17-18).

Although they beg comparison, Cecil Brown's sardonic *The Life and Loves of Mr. Jiveass Nigger* is decidedly different from Dany Laferriere's racy *How to Make Love to A Negro*. Nevertheless, both novels portray a certain attitude about Cool Jazz, interracial sex, mysticism, free love (or promiscuity), the politics of division, sexual fantasies, and nihilism, as well as similar philosophies of life. These are extremely important things to keep in mind as we try to understand the sickness of the dominant society and the motivations of the black protagonists in each novel. Brown and Laferriere create such complex and authentic worlds around each of their infinitely sad characters that you either root for or loathe them.

Not surprisingly, there are times in both books with the intimate details and explicit sex scenes, which might be too much for some readers; some would even say that both novels are pornographic. Moreover, it must be made abundantly clear that to concern ourselves *only* with sex is an almost fatalistic way of looking at life today, especially in these times of sexually transmitted and incurable diseases. However, the emphasis on unadulterated sex, growing old, opportunism, a search for oneself (or being), pot smoking, greed, loneliness, seclusion, confusion, selfishness, and an absolute dedication to the absurd is quite poignant. Writes Cecil Brown:

> Camus was one of the first white men to realize the coming decline of Western man, yet his stuff about the absurd man is something black people have known for hundreds of years. [And a black man's] absurdity is never more apparent than in [his] relationship with women, white women (165).

Yet from a reader or novelist's perspective, these controversial and engrossing stories abound with philosophical and important black folklore, sexual myths and dreams, improvisations, eloquent anecdotes, original ideas on religion and deep passion, as well as robust and mindless sexual experiences that clearly define the nature and aesthetics of the two similar works. *How to Make Love to A Negro*, therefore, poignantly conveys:

> When you mix black [men] and white [women] you get blood red. With his own woman the black man might not be worth the paper he's printed on, but with a white woman, the chances of something happening are good. Why? Because sexuality is based on fantasy and the black man/white woman fantasy is one of the most explosive ones around (94).

Although these strikingly original and riotous novels can also be considered works of ribald fancy and imagination, with their seemingly contentious beliefs and superstition—maybe passed on by oral tradition—both are based on the reality of black and white sexual relationships in the world today. This is to say, we can view both works as complicated and philosophical doctrines of sexual guilt, remorse, or satiric examinations of the preposterous, as well as documents of the love-hate relationships between whites and blacks. According to Laferriere, for instance, "In the sexual act, hatred is more effective than love" (19).

Much less apparent in both works, however, are the attitudes and feelings that many black men perhaps have for white men in general. In fact, and equally revealing, "the white man, except for a few cameos, is virtually absent" from both novels (Early xvii). Nonetheless, as eminent sociologist Calvin C. Hernton once persuasively argued, which is germane to our discussion:

> The white man's self-esteem is in a constant state of sexual anxiety in all matters dealing with race relations. So is the [black man's], because his life, too,

is enmeshed in the absurd system of racial hatred in America. Since racism is
centered in and revolves around sex, the [black man] cannot help but see
himself as at once sexually affirmed and negated (7).

It may suffice to point out that whatever fears and sexual hang-ups and
limitations we face in society today, a preoccupation with sex will remain a
part of the love-hate paradigm of white and black relations. In other words,
expounding upon sex and racial dynamics will always fascinate (or titillate)
many Americans. Toward this end, Brown misses no opportunity in *The Life
and Loves of Mr. Jiveass Nigger* to explain his main character's sexual exploits—
a procession of sexual liaisons and meaningless trysts or one-night stands—in
a 'permissive world' of white women prior to the advent of the AIDS virus.
His provocative and cerebral novel, of course, is also grounded in the world
of black protest fiction, like Richard Wright's famous book, *Native Son* (1940).
About this particular brand of black protest, Brown once stated that, "the
white man's concept of protest, which is that of a raging, ferocious, uncool,
demoralized black boy banging on the immaculate door of White Society
begging, not so much for political justice as for his own identity, and in the
process consuming himself, [means] that in the final analysis, his destiny is at
the mercy of the White Man" (Fuller, 346).

Additionally, or to put it another way, National Book Award winner and
MacArthur Genius Award recipient, Charles Johnson, writing in *Being and
Race*, reminds us that when *The Life and Loves of Mr. Jiveass Nigger* was pub-
lished in 1969, it

> received a good deal of attention.... At bottom, it's a sometimes funny sex
> farce about a black American named George Washington seducing, and being
> seduced, in Copenhagen before he realizes he must return home to help in the
> struggle for racial progress (91-92).

Perhaps it is a surprise then that Brown's celebrated first book is also
devoted to the burlesque, and ridiculous, given the particular scandalous and
teaser title, and that he achieves the effect of entertaining us (readers) through
ridicule, innuendo, black legend, unusual forms, caricature, skillful literary in-
vention, and comical distortions, as well as the imparting of a parody and
entree of literary styles. Even more important, Brown's powerfully raw narrative shows flashes of brilliance, even with the numerous sexual affairs with
wayward white women.

The New York Times, for example, commenting exuberantly on the noto-
rious book, wrote *The Life and Loves of Mr. Jiveass Nigger* is "flimflamboyantly

erotic…audacious…dramatic…. Mr. Brown is a born pornographer gone straight" (Brown). In essence, Brown's understanding of humanity, black/white sexuality, evil, discrimination, drug lust, racism and power should rank among the most important risqué literary works, such as William Burroughs' *Naked Lunch* (1959), or Jerzy Kosinski's *The Painted Bird* (1965).

Furthermore, writing in the introduction to *How to Make Love to A Negro*, French translator David Homel boldly asserts that "The coupling of white women and [black men] creates a lot of sparks—the attraction of opposites, the potency of guilt, the weight of history" (9). And as far as the historical and sexual record and conflict of blacks and whites in America is concerned, black sociologist Hernton writes:

> The sexualization of racism in the United States is a unique phenomenon in the history of mankind, [as] it is an anomaly of the first order. In fact, there is a sexual involvement, at once real and vicarious, connecting white and black people in America that spans the history of this country from the era of slavery to the present, an involvement so immaculate and yet so perverse, so ethereal and yet so concrete, that all race relations tend to be, however subtle, *sex* relations (7).

Consequently, the un-named hero in Laferriere's widely acclaimed novel is comparable to novelist Ralph Ellison's great novel *Invisible Man* (1952), in that it tries to deal with the realities of the insane world around him, and the black-white paradigm, as the main character in Laferriere's work also feels irresistibly compelled to have sex for sport with any and all willing (mostly educated) white women (preferably attending McGill University in Canada). Laferriere's hero is notoriously promiscuous, as is his truly weird black room-mate and self proclaimed guru and Jazz aficionado, Bouba, who always sleeps, eats, and has *coitus* on the front room's rumpled and smelly couch (of their roach-infested apartment at 3670 rue St.-Denis), dispensing vague or supposedly sage advice about Sigmund Freud, John Coltrane, Miles Davis, our corruptible world, and Allah, as well as the benefits of spiritual sex, or sexual healing, divine orgasms, and the mysteries of black life. Laferriere also cogently explains:

> Bouba is a true hermit. He can spend whole days without even turning on the light. The day passes; Bouba meditates and prays. He wishes to become the purest among pure men. He intends to accept the challenge issued to Muhammad: 'You cannot make the deaf hear, nor can you guide the blind or those who are in gross error.' Sure xliii, 39 (22-23).

I think it is also important to point out that in Brown's novel, another self-declared spiritual teacher or sex-addict and confidence man, Bob Jacobs, a sort of 'walking phallus,' is actually introduced—matter-of-factly—as a black hair dresser in *Life and Loves of Mr. Jiveass Nigger*. Our black protagonist, George Washington (alias Paul Winthrop, Jr., Anthony, Julius Makewell, and Efan) holds the sexual predator, Bob, in overwhelming awe, because he surpasses him in infidelity and fervor when it comes to pursuing, in earnest, white women for gratis and gratuitous sex and games. Brown tells us:

> George admired Bob's profession of lover, because the black lover was a true warrior, a true soldier who is doomed, cursed, to fighting a perpetual battle with an elusive enemy, and with the foreknowledge that he can never be the victor, and fighting everyday with this foreknowledge that he can never be the victor makes him victorious every moment of his life. His only security being in knowing that, as a black man, there is no security. Not as long as the world is the way it is (121-122).

Perhaps another source of interpretive complexity is that Brown's *The Life and Loves of Mr. Jiveass Nigger* and Laferriere's *How to Make Love to A Negro* pontificate and philosophize about death and dying—quite similar worlds or familiar territory in both works. Speaking generally of death and the specific act of sexual intercourse, Laferriere ventures, "We sense their movements in a mad modern ballet. Two naked bodies violently intertwined in a *pas de deux* of death..." (38). He goes on to reflect, "Black and white are equal when it comes to death and sexuality" (49). Similarly, Brown writes:

> George said that it's when I lie down that I think of death...and that when I'm up walking around it's like I'll never die. Lying down is a kind of symbolic death, and so is fucking, which must be the soul of death, and dreaming (118).

The idea of dying during the sex act, then becomes a sort of metaphor for a 'living death,' and as Brown expresses it, living off your *insides* (213). Indeed, the more one performs the sex act with multiple partners, or strangers, the closer he or she comes to ritualistic death, or perhaps righteous enlightenment, and life. So in this sense, both books are preoccupied with sex and death. In either case, the leading characters in both novels use athletic sex to escape from immediate problems, the growing disgust with most of the life around them, the white world, and the realities of existence. Ironically, Laferriere laments, "Making love to a Negro isn't frightening; sleeping with him is. Sleeping is complete surrender. It's more than nude; it's naked. Anything can happen during the night, when reason sleeps. Do we dream our lover? Do we penetrate his dreams?" (62)

All in all, we should not be led to believe—by Brown or Laferriere's irreverent and iconoclastic writings—that such uninhibited behavior and sexual recklessness are something that should be expected, imitated, or desired from an intimate and long-term monogamous relationship. As Julian Mayfield informs us:

> Intelligence alone ought to reject the notion that the Black Aesthetic has anything to do with [blacks] supposed super-sexuality...for this is a myth in which both blacks and whites believe with an unshakable faith as solid as the Rock of Ages. One supposes that the myth can do no harm as long as it helps us to groove in the night and achieve or produce the maximum number of orgasms, which is our national obsession (25).

Therefore, in a way, one can say that Brown's and Laferriere's outrageous and convoluted books are devoid of any ethical elements, pathos, or sexual morality. To understand this assertion even more clearly, we must consider Professor Gerald Early's searching introduction to the Ecco Press edition of *The Life and Loves of Mr. Jiveass Nigger*. Early succinctly writes that the novel gives us,

> a portrait of a predatory world where sex is the only mode of expression, money the only value, lies the only language, opportunism the only faith. The novel may take place in Copenhagen...but the perverse culture depicted here seems particularly a critique of America (xvii).

Laferriere also focuses upon, as Early puts it, "the sexual phantasmagoria of black men and white women" (xvii). In other words, the books show parallels between the rites of passage of the so-called 'invincible' black and white youth, and the perverse beliefs of sexual adventurism. Cecil Brown, who recently earned his Ph.D. in Folklore, Narrative, and African-American Literature from Berkeley, has achieved great notoriety for his *The Life and Loves of Mr. Jiveass Nigger*, as it became an instant bestseller, ostensibly because astute readers, black intellectuals, and the black masses of the younger generation can relate to the story of a black expatriate mired in the lives of (un)sophisticated white Europeans, without equivocations or pretense.

Further, Laferriere's rogue tale of interracial sex and drugs, including episodes of a dreary life in Canada—that is, living as a black immigrant—is also totally believable, especially as it serves up an edgy criticism and attraction for the sexual freedom with uninhibited Anglo Saxon women in a foreign and exotic land of whites. Perhaps this is apparently part of the lure for black men. As a consequence, both authors' profound and sometimes superficial views tend to lose sight of reality, and the self or 'being' and the real purpose of their fragmented characters' lives.

Indeed, by another measure, there is no real search for the truth by these unsavory or pathetic and comic characters in the raw stories. Nevertheless, Brown's work, *The Life and Loves of Mr. Jiveass Nigger*, enables him to transmit or extol ideas about black aesthetics and contemporary social issues, as well as American racial problems. Moreover, David Homel points out that Laferriere:

> knows about the totality of America from the underside. Born in Port-au-Prince [Haiti], he practiced journalism under Duvalier. When a colleague with whom he was working on a story [in 1978] was found murdered by the roadside, Laferriere took the hint and went into exile in Canada (8).

It hardly needs to be said that the depraved lives of the two main characters in each book become ultimately what they essentially make of things and themselves. This is particularly true if one believes he or she is responsible for the personal and social consequences of his own actions. George Washington, in *The Life and Loves of Mr. Jiveass Nigger*, tries hard to make radical changes in himself. But, of course, for George Washington, sexual adventure and voyeurism become a journey of discovery in itself. Professor Early, however, would perhaps disagree with this contention, as he believes Brown's book, in the end, has no redeeming social or moral value; and therefore, George Washington ultimately fails in his relations with women, because:

> *The Life and Loves of Mr. Jiveass Nigger* is a portrait of a world without a human center, without the coherence of human commitment. It is, indeed, nothing more than the world of confidence men. In this regard, this novel is as dark as anything written by Chester Himes, who greatly influenced it, or as nightmarish a vision of human nature as anything by Iceberg Slim, whose work is contemporaneous with this novel (xviii).

It must be clearly understood, however, that Chester Himes not only influenced Brown's book, but also he praised it highly and repeatedly before his death in Spain in 1984. Equally important, we must recognize that both Brown and Laferriere have perhaps learned from the novels of previous African American writers, such as James Baldwin's *Another Country* (1962) and

Tell Me How Long The Train's Been Gone (1968), where he addressed particular issues of sexual and racial politics, or the anti-white aesthetics of Ishmael Reed's *The Freelance Pallbearers* (1967), and *Mumbo Jumbo* (1976), or John A. William's journalistically accurate account of the destructive black/white sex and power relationships in *The Man Who Cried I Am* (1967).

Moreover, we must consider the early satirical and legendary strange or weird works of Hal Bennett, and Clarence Majors, or finally, George S. Schuyler's attack on the myths of racial purity and white supremacy in *Black No More* (1931), which are also pioneering and relevant. Currently, certain modern-day black writers, like Terry McMillan, especially in her second book, *Disappearing Acts* (1989), or Charles Johnson's *Middle Passage* (1933), which is about nineteenth century American master-slave sexuality, also show the influence of Cecil Brown and the aforementioned great black writers.

Whatever limitations the two novels by Brown and Laferriere may have, they are extremely important, eclectic, streetwise documentaries of the complexity of black life, giving us savory reading entertainment. Both books are successful at conveying a particular place, time, and subject, making us think critically about sex and race. Distinguished scholar and African American sociologist Dr. Winthrop D. Jordan has posited that the dynamics of interracial sex:

> has been and remains absolutely central to race relations in this country. The tensions inherent in interracial sex have constituted pervasive and persistent themes in our history. And not only in our past. Anyone in this country who has walked publicly arm in arm with a person of the opposite sex and race can testify that old hostilities are not yet dead. Indeed there are not many Americans, black or white, who can *honestly* say that they have no emotional reaction to such *implied* interracial sexuality—the point being that our eyes view a fully clad couple and, because the couple is interracial, our minds immediately disrobe them and...pop them into bed, there to work out whatever particular fantasies our own backgrounds and personalities suggest (10).

Both *The Life and Loves of Mr. Jiveass Nigger* and *How to Make Love to A Negro*, I believe, have important moral messages, and relevant literary value, starting with the ethos—or pornographic pathos of black men, as well as providing a serious dialogue on sexual politics and racial matters throughout the world today. Furthermore, by understanding the literary nuances and fantastical mode of storytelling, historical underpinnings of sex and race, and the unique rhythm or cadence of language and communication experiments in both prophetic books, as well as their intellectual frameworks and unparalleled insights, we can perhaps empower ourselves about such lewd and controversial subject matters.

To be sure, as Hernton correctly surmised back in 1965, "The sexualization of the race problem is a reality, and we are going to have to deal with it even though most of us are, if not unwilling, definitely unprepared" (5). This will be especially true for the writing of black risque fiction in the future. In the final analysis, both of these thoughtful and compelling books leave an intellectual legacy and have made important and lasting contributions to the genre of African American literature.

REFERENCES

Brown, Cecil. 1969. *The Life and Loves of Mr. Jiveass Nigger.* New York: Fawcett Crest Book.

Early, Gerald. 1991. Introduction: *The Life and Loves of Mr. Jiveass Nigger* by Cecil Brown. New York: The Ecco Press.

Fuller, Hoyt W. 1972. "The New Black Literature: Protest or Affirmation." *The Black Aesthetic.* Ed. Addison Gayle, Jr. New York: Anchor Books.

Hernton, Calvin C. 1965. *Sex and Racism in America.* New York: Grove Press, Inc.

Homel, David. 1987. Introduction: *How to Make Love to A Negro*, by Dany Laferriere. London: Bloomsbury Publishing, Ltd.

Johnson, Charles. 1988. *Being and Race: Black Writing Since 1970.* Indianapolis: Indiana University Press.

Jordan, Winthrop D. Introduction: *Black/White Sex*, by Grace Halsell. Greenwich, Connecticut: A Fawcett Crest Book.

Laferriere, Dany. 1987. *How to Make Love to A Negro.* Trans. David Homel. London: Bloomsbury Publishing, Ltd.

Mayfield, Julian. 1972. "You Touch My Black Aesthetic and I'll Touch Yours." *The Black Aesthetic.* Ed. Addison Gayle, Jr. New York: Anchor Books.

American Popular Culture and the Politics of Race in Dr. Seuss' *The Sneetches*

THE BEGINNING

Cartoons, particularly editorial or political cartoons, make use of specific elements of caricature to explain or make light of current politics and social issues. Caricatures in American picture storybooks are satirical, sometimes bizarre foolishness—plastic representations, or descriptions—which through gross exaggeration of natural features, make cartoon characters appear ridiculous, while also trying to make clear a particular point of view.

Some picture storybooks about politics also try to explain troubling social issues, giving a somewhat realistic or embellished representation of the obvious facts. According to Professor Roger A. Fisher, "By its very nature, political cartoon art in a democratic society has been one of the purest artifacts of popular culture, seeking to influence public opinion through its use of widely and instantly understood symbols, slogans, referents, and allusions" (1996, p. 122).

Humorous cartoons, therefore, have been an integral part of our journalism, the media, and American popular culture. Non-political cartoons, moreover, have become enormously popular with the development of the color funny papers of major newspapers and printed book presses.

Perhaps the greatest and most distinctive cartoon picture book illustrator for children in America was Theodor Geisel, better known as the fictitious Dr. Seuss. Indeed, Dr. Seuss' inimitable artwork and wit have had a profound influence on contemporary American popular culture, and his quaint and outrageous ideas have given a new dimension to the cartoon picture storybook. In fact, Dr. Seuss or Theodor Geisel, as a children's book author, "revolutionized the very idea of what writing for children should be, and [he] wrote and illustrated over forty world famous books" (Sendak, 1995). Furthermore, Dr. Seuss' expressive and daffy drawings and unfettered imagination and work expanded to include important political and thoughtful social commentary as well as personal satire. A 1999 *Wall Street Journal* editorial explained, moreover, that:

> Although Dr. Seuss won fame with sweetly screwball drawings and catchy rhymes, his venture into political cartooning should not surprise those familiar with his children's books, which often carried serious, politically liberal messages. (1999, p. B9C)

FLIGHTS OF FANCY

Dr. Seuss' work, which has had enormous appeal, and is still popular today, is basically meant for children, but many of his odd stories, like *The Sneetches*, are also suitable for adult understanding and entertainment and are inextricably a part of our cultural landscape. In other words, *The Sneetches*, a landmark in illustrated cartoon books, which turns weird pictures into a strange story, is intended to instruct not only children but adults as well about the problems of being prejudiced or different. In fact, Dr. Seuss' penchant for wry humor and his ability to starkly explain how discrimination—and even racism—can adversely affect individuals and *all* Americans remains unsurpassed.

Dr. Seuss creates a visual frame of reference or framework through his amusing and quirky characters, and the fallacy of being intolerant and prejudiced against others comes vividly to life. Dr. Seuss' framework can best be explained by Professors Lucius J. Barker, Mack H. Jones, and Katherine Tate, as they write:

> A frame of reference is a set of general assumptions about the nature of the subject or experience being investigated, what concepts or categories of analysis are the most useful for understanding it, what level of analysis should be adopted, and what questions should be answered in order to develop the most useful understanding of that [which] is being investigated. (1999, p. 5)

Dr. Seuss' assumptions and intentions are clearly outlined at the beginning of his sassy story of *The Sneetches*. In addition, Dr. Seuss' wildly imaginative and satirical account of the sociopolitical conditions of our time, notably the intractable problems of race and human differences, is especially informative. Indeed, his vibrant comic portrait of *The Sneetches* intensifies his dramatization of the stated issues. Moreover, his interdependent and colorful text and grotesque or unusual illustrations of the funny-looking, beak-nosed Sneetches—who appear as yellow, upright-walking ducks on steroids—are given equal emphasis with the story's telling and didactic language, which also enhances the text's explainability. For example, Dr. Seuss (1989, p. 3) writes:

> Now, the Star Belly Sneetches
> Had bellies with stars.
> The Plain-Belly Sneetches
> Had none upon thars.
> Those stars weren't so big.
> They were really so small.
> You might think such a thing
> Wouldn't matter at all.

Nonetheless, the Star-Belly Sneetches became a distinct and dominant group in the society of beach Sneetches. And in this sense, Dr. Seuss, a seemingly sophisticated cartoonist for children, describes how one race or species can dehumanize others by pressing forward the supposed superiority of their own kind, as did the arrogant Star-Belly Sneetches in this story. Perhaps they attributed this to their higher cultural and psychological values. Further, the intolerance and bias of the cantankerous Star-Belly Sneetches are easily substantiated by their unfavorable opinion and prejudgment of the Plain-Belly Sneetches.

On this note, it is interesting to point out Dr. Seuss' excellent molding and blending of words and cross-cultural analysis and comparison of the different Sneetches. He asserts that the distinguishing characteristics of the Star-Belly Sneetches are a product of their enthnocentricism. This Dr. Seuss believes, is why the Sneetches with stars fear and are uncomfortable with the Plain-Belly Sneetches—that is, those particular misfits who do not look like them or fit their image. And if it is also true that the Sneetches without stars are uncomfortable or are at least ambivalent about their separate and miserable existence, would it be surprising to think that the Plain-Belly Sneetches perhaps hated themselves, or even wanted to be like the Star-Belly Sneetches, their cursed rivals or contemporaries.

Of course, throughout history, unrestrained discrimination, preconceived notions or separatism, and prejudices have caused a fair amount of pain and human suffering. Therefore, by examining the hostility that the Plain-Belly

Sneetches engendered, perhaps one can understand the unwanted discrimination many minorities still face in America. In the sophisticated and moving Sneetches story, one is classified or stereotyped and unfairly judged on the basis of having a star on his or her stomach, which tells us about their exact physiological traits.

THE POLITICS OF RACE

For that matter, what exactly is race or the basic physical characteristics of all humans? Science writer James C. King tells us that, "the concept of race is an attempt to describe the manner in which individual variation within and between populations is related to heredity, development, and environment" (1981, p. ix). This definition, however, does not explain precisely how the members of one so-called race prefer *only* themselves over others. Biologically or genetically speaking, race doesn't really exist. According to science writer Kim A. McDonald, "an analysis of three types of human genes that reveal the patterns of human evolution for the past million years concludes that race has nothing to do with the historical sublineages of humanity" (1998, p. A19). More importantly, as the influential public intellectual Ashley Montagu has written, "The idea of "race" represents one of the most dangerous myths of our time, and one of the most tragic" (1997, p. 41).

Incredible though it seems, Dr. Seuss explains the characteristics of *The Sneetches* with grandeur and dignity, while pointing out the detrimental effect of 'same-kind' preference. Toward this end, we must understand that race and racism have been analyzed by numerous scholars, most of whom view it as an irrational form of behavior. It is based on the need to identify scapegoats like the Plain-Belly Sneetches to justify their snobbish existence and irrational hatred and aggression against others, perhaps to relieve their racial guilt or inferiority complex. The Star-Belly Sneetches' action also tends to be in a *consonant* direction. However, one must ask: Can terrible guilt drive a curmudgeon Sneetch or human person mad?

The Star-Belly Sneetches' resentments are gradually replaced by feelings of extreme prejudice, stemming from the notion that the Plain-Belly Sneetches are a distinctly different and supposedly inferior sub-group of Sneetches. The unpopularity of the Plain-Belly Sneetches, on whom unfairness and all sorts of evils could be blamed, with impunity—and where they are sporadically persecuted and personally restricted—is quite evident in this outlandish story. For instance, Dr. Seuss explains:

When the Star-Belly Sneetches had frankfurter roasts or picnics or parties or marshmallow toasts, they never invited the Plain-Belly Sneetches. They left them out cold, in the dark of the beaches. They kept them away. Never let them come near. And that's how they treated them year after year. (1989, p. 7)

Although contact has been made among the races in the United States to a certain degree through the painful process of integration—to reduce elements of prejudice and discrimination, especially in establishing common, nationalistic goals—it is through *political socialization* and improper learning that we reject our fellow brethren, like the Plain-Belly Sneetches' repudiation by the Star-Belly Sneetches. And this attitude became prevalent and incorporated into their Sneetch-Beach society.

Moreover, indirect personal or tactile contact between the Sneetches—like in human society—is not effective in reducing the Star-Belly Sneetches, prejudices, as they continue to discriminate against the Plain-Belly Sneetches. This is important to understand, because some iconoclastic scholars have claimed that racism, prejudices, and discrimination are permanent. For example, Professor Derrick Bell, in support of this thesis, has succinctly written:

[Minorities] will never gain full equality in this country. Even those Herculean efforts we hail as successful will produce no more than temporary "peaks of progress," short-lived victories that slide into irrelevance as racial patterns adapt in ways that maintain white dominance. This is a hard-to-accept fact that all history verifies. We must acknowledge it, not as a sign of submission, but as an act of ultimate defiance. (1992, p. 12)

If Bell's dire assertions are correct, attempts to chronicle or explain the motivation of those who hate and perpetuate our racial problems are critically important. Dr. Seuss' thesis regarding the Sneetches must be examined, and considered, if for no other reason than to explain how children (or the offspring from adults) can learn this same kind of destructive and counterproductive behavior over successive generations.

The Star-Belly Sneetches' form of hatred and displeasure ranges initially from intolerance to disgust and is based solely on the dislike they have of the Sneetches without "stars on thars." However, in an effort to be more like the dominant Sneetches, the Plain-Belly Sneetches took action to 'remake' themselves through the magical machinations of a visiting outsider, namely, Sylvester McMonkey McBean, and his wonderful and peculiar Star-On, Star-Off Machines.

Beside looking like Dr. Seuss' gray, cat-like and mean-spirited Grinch that stole Christmas, in Whoville, the cunning McBean, who gives an immediate impression of deviousness, was able to artificially produce the same brilliant stars on the Star-less Belly Sneetches, much to the chagrin of the original Star-Belly Sneetches. Afterward, when the fantastic deed was done, the disparaged and former Plain-Belly Sneetches happily and boisterously proclaimed:

> We're exactly like you! You can't tell us apart. We're all just the same, now, you snooty old smarties! And now we can go to your frankfurter parties. (Seuss, 1989, p. 12)

African Americans and other minorities have long tried to change, like the Plain-Belly Sneetches, to adapt to remake themselves and work within the constraints of the dominant society. However, it seems there are those who can't stand to see others get ahead—or to share power. In essence, not all people are treated the same way. The fact of the matter is, our society restricts those who are different from the dominant group.

Indeed, the attainment of stars on the former Plain-Belly Sneetches did not mean the end of their problems or persecution. Therefore, removing the source of the problem, or changing oneself, does not always mean a reduction in prejudice or discrimination. Sometimes it takes a change in attitude.

This is why the resentful, undaunted Star-Belly Sneetches, for a considerable monetary price charged by the wily and shifty Sylvester McMonkey McBean, decided, in turn, to remove their famous Belly Stars, saying wistfully and defiantly, "We're *still* the best Sneetches and they [the former Plain-Belly Sneetches] are the worst" (Seuss, 1989, p. 13).

This part of Dr. Seuss' story illustrates accurately the burden many minorities are faced with when they try to advance socially in the dominant culture, or to be accepted, as they are sometimes pulled back down, marginalized, or knocked off their hard-earned perch. The Plain-Belly Sneetches can perhaps relate to this. After the original Star-Belly Sneetches finally had their illustrious stars removed by McBean's Star-Off Machine, they bragged and "paraded about...with snouts in the air." indignantly stating:

> We know who is who! Now there isn't a doubt. The best kind of Sneetches are Sneetches without! (Seuss, 1989, p. 18)

Taking advantage of the situation, the happy-go-lucky rogue, McBean, after cleverly bargaining and taking all of the unsuspecting Sneetches' money, concluded that the simple-minded, beak-nosed populace that "lived on the beaches," would never learn, or be willing to tolerate each other, because of their vanity and self-hatred. And as the sly Sylvester McMonkey McBean drove away in his splendid and sensational car and Star-On, Star-Off Machines, he amusingly declared to himself, "No. You can't teach a Sneetch!" (Seuss, 1989, p. 22)

CONCLUSION

Having lost most of their wealth, and despite words to the contrary, the indomitable Sneetches finally realized that it really didn't matter if they were different. In Dr. Seuss' optimistic words:

> ...McBean was quite wrong. I'm quite happy to say that the Sneetches got really quite smart on that day, the day they decided that Sneetches are Sneetches, and no kind of Sneetch is the best on the beaches. That day, all the Sneetches forgot about stars and whether they had one, or not, upon thars. (1989, p. 24)

Will such a day in human history and race relations ever come? Dr. Seuss' zany and irresistible Sneetch characters reveal his careful observation and analysis of race, especially for the future in America. He takes the position that a significant difference does exist between us all, although his wacky sensibilities playfully tell us that we should never be afraid to address or entertain the question of race in the United States.

It is this later discussion at the very end of the principal book, *The Sneetches*, which is one of the most interesting parts of the eccentric story. The late Dr. Seuss managed to explore the question of race, and race-related problems, polarizing racial politics, and intolerance in our heterogeneous society. Nonetheless, tolerance prevailed in the story in the end.

More importantly, Dr. Seuss challenges our basic assumptions—that we cannot get past our prejudices, or transcend race—and that discrimination is insignificant. According to Professor Charles V. Willie, of Harvard Graduate School of Education, "it is all a matter of perspective" (1978, p. 10). Willie goes on to write, "From the perspective of the dominant people of power, *inequality* exists because of the personal inadequacies of those who are less fortunate" (1978, p. 10). Fortunately, however, as Professor King, in *The Biology of Race*, has pointed out:

> During the past two decades the United States has become officially committed to policies of racial integration in education and of fostering equality of civil rights and economic opportunity for all citizens. These policies constitute a clear repudiation of many [prejudicial] practices of the past and run counter to the beliefs of large segments of the population. (1981, p. ix)

Finally, anyone who reads the off-the-wall, but morality-filled and plausible *The Sneetches*, should feel that the story and its moral are timeless. In terms of human comprehension and human interaction or intervention, one would have to conclude that the question of race and racism will always be a part of American culture. However, it does not mean that in a diverse society such as ours, we can't get along and work together as a cohesive whole, and as part of the human race. In short, we are all humans—the same people—regardless of our color, racial, religious and cultural differences.

REFERENCES

Barker, Lucius J., Mack H. & Tate, Katherine. 1999. *African Americans and the American Political System*. 4th edition. New Jersey: Prentice Hall, Inc.

Bell, Derrick. 1992. *Faces at the Bottom of the Well: The Permanence of Racism*. New York: Basic Books.

"Dr. Seuss Drawings Depict Fight Against Fascism." 1999, August 16. *The Wall Street Journal*.

Fisher, Roger A. 1996. *Them Damned Pictures: Explorations in American Political Cartoon Art*. North Haven, Connecticut: Archon Books.

King, James C. 1981. *The Biology of Race*. Revised Edition. Los Angeles, California: University Press.

McDonald, Kim A. 1998, October 30. "Genetically Speaking, Race Doesn't Exist." *The Chronicle of Higher Education*. p. A19.

Montagu, Ashley. 1997. *Man's Most Dangerous Myth: The Fallacy of Race*. 6th edition. Walnut Creek, California: Alta Mira Press.

The Secret Art of Dr. Seuss. 1995. Introduction by Maurice Sendak. New York: Random House.

The Sneetches and Other Stories. 1989. Dr. Seuss, catalogued by the Library of Congress as Geisel, Theodor Seuss. New York: Random House.

Willie, Charles V. 1978. "The Inclining Significance of Race." *Society*. Vol. 15, No. 3, p. 10-15.

Origins of the American Race War of 2010

The letter that follows is a frightening and darkly prophetic and imaginative excursion into a possible and terrible future. A race war has taken place in the United States of America—the year is 2010—and the retired African American General, Freeman Beckwith, the second black man in the armed forces to become the Chairman of the Joint Chiefs of Staff in 2006, has taken complete control of the southern states of Louisiana, Tennessee, Mississippi, Alabama, and Georgia. He has declared himself the President of the New African Republic and announced the formal secession from the United States of America.

This American race war scenario is speculative, a written device to voice my fear of the chilling possibilities and serious concerns over contemporary social and political issues affecting our nation, especially in terms of our voluntary polarization and racial divisions. Moreover, it is not a prediction of things to come, but my personal take on why and how such a race war could or might occur in the United States in the near future.

Finally, before the author's execution by the U.S. federal government, a hand-written, hundred-page letter (call it a confession) is published in *The New York Times* and is presented here verbatim. I can only hope that this cautionary tale will be viewed for its potential for educating all Americans about the possibilities of a racial war that we can ill afford as a multi-ethnic (or racial) society. Otherwise, it will be to our inestimable detriment.

December 30, 2010

Hello, Youngblood,

So you are still alive? That was good news. I was glad to hear this from my white prison handlers. Particularly since our whole family, "our people" have been almost wiped out, annihilated. As an up-and-coming Lieutenant Colonel, and former aide to General Beckwith, I had it made. But I am now as known as the Black Judas, or the Uncle Tommy Negro who sold out The Black General—that is, after I had been captured upon escaping from Beckwith's secret military headquarters in Mississippi. But I told them nothing, blood. After all, I surrendered.

As you know by now, I am imprisoned at the Federal Prison Camp, at Nellis Airbase in the state of Nevada, for my so-called active participation and role in the modern-day civil rebellion, or tragedy, and I wait now on death row, as I will eventually be put to death for my supposed crimes of sedition and treason.

I am allowed to have research materials, the use of books from the prison library, magazines, newspapers, pens and paper, and other writing utensils. By the way, my court appointed attorney has promised to mail this letter to you—at the federal detention center in Chicago—after I am dead and gone. Youngblood, I was told that over 500,000 black men, women and children are warehoused there for rioting, looting, fighting, and mostly sympathizing with General Beckwith in the South. So they are political prisoners. The federal government still don't know what to do with them. As I understand it, many blacks, including Hip-Hop artists and Gangsta Rappers tried unsuccessfully to join General Beckwith's rebel forces.

I was also told that blacks from federal and state prisons across the nation would be released only if they chose to fight as soldiers on the front lines against General Beckwith. And, if they somehow lived, they would again earn their freedom or be pardoned, and their crimes wiped from existence or expunged from the proverbial record.

Anyway, my main purpose in writing this letter to you is to explain the "Origins of the American Race War of 2010," now that it is almost over. No doubt, it will go down in the annals as the worst incident of racial violence in the United States history. I sometimes wonder if Henry Fuller, the President of the United States was serious about what he recently said—that is, the federal government would not give in to "blackmail" by black revolutionary thugs.

Do you know that Fuller also vowed on network television to destroy the so-called New African American Republic, hunt down its black leaders; and mount full-scale combat operations against them? Finally, he said that there was no possibility of a truce in the conflict with the break-away, nationalist, anti-federal black government. But would he give the go-ahead to drop nuclear weapons on General Beckwith's headquarters in Mississippi, if it was found? I hope not.

As you know, having even the semblance of an independent Black State (or a separate racial enclave) within the nation had been the U.S. bogeyman since the beginning of the Race War. The United States government accused General Beckwith of plotting (from the start) an unnecessary rebellion among angry, disgruntled, and restless blacks and vowed that he would be eventually tried and hanged for treason.

I suppose the Race War of 2010 was actually the result of racial hatred, complacency, lingering racism, and the gradual apathy on the part of *all* American citizens, who, more or less, gave tacit approval of the deteriorating racial climate, as well as trends identified as far back as 1995. First, we permitted dangerous organized hate groups and militant white racists to persist and flourish, saying that not giving them the right to exist would violate their First Amendment Rights. That was a mistake.

Second, we allowed angry, hateful and like-minded rogues to run rampart in our society, unafraid and unchecked, to randomly kill—no, murder—blacks, Jews, and other minorities at will. Why did our government ignore these sick bigots and terrorists? Perhaps it was because our *pathetic* political leaders repeatedly turned away from the responsibility of controlling—no, stopping—such menacing and dangerous psychopaths.

Columnist Pam Adams wrote in 1999 that "White men commit more mass murders; therefore, all white men are suspect; therefore, skin color [should have been] cause for [some kind of] suspicion" (p. 9B). African American psychiatrists William H. Grier and Price Cobbs also suggested in 1968 that black Americans should "maintain a high degree of suspicion toward the motives of every white man and at the same time never allow this suspicion to impair [their] grasp of reality" (Grier & Cobbs, 1968, p. 135). But these profoundly disturbing facts and information were summarily ignored. Perhaps no one wanted to panic society at large.

But what could blacks have done exactly? African American Columnist Clarence Page also asked why we "simply remain silent while others attacked?" [He went on]: "When justice hangs in the balance, the silent people can be the most dangerous of all" (1999, p. 3D). Maybe there was some truth in what Page wrote. The brilliant African American psychiatrist, Alvin F. Poussaint also suggested back in 1999 that the American Psychiatric Association, as well as our government, should:

designate extreme racism as a mental health problem. [Furthermore], clinicians need guidelines for recognizing delusional racism in all its stages so that they can provide treatment. Otherwise, racists will continue to fall through the cracks of the mental health system, and we can expect more of them to act out their deadly delusions. (Poussaint, 1999, p. A21)

Columnist Page took issue with Dr. Poussaint's prescription, however, when he wrote that, "racial bigotry can manifest itself in mental illness. Some bigots could use some serious mental help. But you don't have to be insane to be a bigot. You just have to learn all the wrong lessons from the normal world around you" (1999, p. 2E).

The American people did not heed Poussaint's dire warning, nor was extreme racism declared a mental health problem. In fact, some hate groups even encouraged violence and deadly behavior. For example, one of the leading young and enterprising white racists of the late 1990s, Matt Hale, leader of the white supremacist World Church of the Creator (WCOTC) advocated the death of all minorities. Hale's antipathy or hatred toward blacks and Jews was unprecedented. Further, Hale was "adept at using the media to espouse a sanitized version of his hatred and to enhance his own celebrity" (Levin, 1999, 15A); but he too believed we would one day have a Racial Holy War, or "RaHoWa," as white racists called it.

What also emerged, as journalist Jo Thomas pointed out, was "a new style of 'leaderless white resistance'—long urged by white supremacist leaders—of very small cells, pairs or individuals called lone wolves, acting independently" (Thomas, 1999, p. A1) to intentionally harm others who were different from whites—projecting their *invidious* discrimination and aggressive behavior. In other words, these white racists hated others who looked different from themselves.

Somehow we should have also been aware or warned of the dangerous message provided by two wealthy racist entrepreneurs, Vincent Bertollini and Carl Story, who financed the white supremacist movement from their Northern Idaho homes for years. The emergence of Bertollini and Story, and their tremendous wealth, which was made in California's computer industry, was frustrating and a blow to our multi-racial democracy because their particular status gave credence to white racists everywhere. They essentially thought white people were "the true Israelites and superior to Jews and nonwhites...and caretakers of the world" (Idaho White Supremacists, 1998, p. 5B).

Furthermore, these specific trends were also the *direct* development of the white militia hate groups, such as the Confederate Knights of America, the Nazi Skin Heads, the National Alliance, the Ku Klux Klan, and new-aged Neo-Nazi groups. Moreover, other radical white supremacist fringe groups, like the National Association for the Advancement of White People or the NAAWP—white supremacist David Duke's venomously spiteful creation— was *evil* incarnate. There was finally the Council of Conservative Citizens (or the CCC), about whom the prolific historical journalist and columnist from the state of Nevada, John L. Smith, had this to say:

> Under the guise of preserving the true heritage of the South, the CCC mimics most intellectual hate groups by opining that white European culture is all that will save the planet. The CCC is known as a hybrid of the old White Citizens councils that had chapters throughout the South during segregationist times. (1999, p. 1B)

This passage by Smith is important to understand because many of the racist hate groups believed that America should be an all-white nation, without exception. In essence, white racists should rule and become the masters of our world. Nonetheless, the original aim of the militia movement in America essentially was "to protect constitutional rights and provide for the nation's defense in times of war or emergency" (FBI, 1999, p. 5A). That original intent, however, was diluted and stood on its head. Moreover, for white racist demagogues, this came to mean the "return [of] political power to the average white American citizen and [to] keep governmental authority out of the hands of the wealthy ruling elite, particularly that small minority [or secret cabal] of Jews" (Neo-Nazi, 1999, p. 8A), and hateful, or disagreeable blacks. Unfortunately, their actions later became reality, and the cross-burnings and indiscriminate lynching (once again) were vigorously "on" for (and against) black men in America, and became a means of "ethnic cleansing" as racist whites came to call it in America in 2008.

We should not forget the black hate groups either, as they became a part of the problem also—such as the Negro Philadelphia Militia; the United Nuwaubian Nation of Moors (who believed in shouting down the racist walls of Jericho), or the Black Knight Demons. We also had other violent hate groups, such as the Black Avengers, United Niggas, the New Black Panther Party, the Black Islamic Muslims, the Black Brotherhood, and the Black Jews of America. Most of America had never heard of these black hate groups because many were secretive or underground.

But do you remember the incendiary Khallid Muhammad of Louis Farrakhan's Nation of Islam? Boy, did he ever upset white America. The flamboyant Muhammad, or the late Harold Moore, Jr., hated white people passionately, intensely—to the core; and he didn't care who knew it. He, of course, often expressed his considerable hatred of whites, Jewish Americans and Uncle Tom Negroes, as he called them. Muhammad preached the racial supremacy of the black man—whom he called the first man—and condemned *any* black person who associated with whites or didn't have so-called racial loyalty.

When former mayor Rudolph Giuliani of New York denounced Khallid Muhammad as a "hatemonger," and his Million Youth March of 1998 as a hate march, Muhammad stated that the white Giuliani was "an ordinary cracker...a devil [who] has no power over [black people]...except the power you gave him" (Smith & Boven, 1998, p. 32). The Black Muslims never forgave Giuliani and fought hard against his bid for United States Senator of New York. Giuliani in turn fought them at every turn and opportunity before he left office in 2001.

Finally, we should not forget the hate-filled Yahweh Ben Yahweh (or God the Son of God in Hebrew) group that resided in Florida. Some believed this virulent and violent black hate group was a sort of cult, or Israelite sect, as they called themselves, whose members believed "blacks are the lost tribe of Israel and the true Jews and that white people are devils" (Former NFL Player, 1999, p. 10A). The group would later advocate or advanced a plan to ship white Americans immediately back to Europe, where they thought whites belonged.

In 1999, the Yahweh Ben Yahweh group was indicted on conspiracy and racketeering charges, as well as for murder (as they committed a series of firebombings, and killed 23 people in the 1980s). They were also convicted on charges of arson and extortion. (Former Football Player, 1999, p. 16B) Yes, Youngblood, it was a sad state of affairs that all these mean-spirited and antagonistic groups were allowed even to exist.

Many of those black militia groups had no use for white people (and from their hate-filled rhetoric, they would just as soon see all whites dead); and many would try to undermine them at any cost and opportunity. To say the least, agonizing death for many by the more vicious black hate groups was an equal opportunity activity, because they would kill both black and white people, or anyone who got in their way, without question. As Clarence Page once wrote, regarding all of these already mentioned groups, "the black hater has much in common with the white hater" (1999, p. 30).

Some said the Race War of 2010 started because of the rolling back of Affirmative Action, and other gains blacks had achieved during the modern-day civil rights movement, but I, for one, never believed these were the only reasons. For example, there were many instances of the severe harassment black people faced (and endured) during the 1990s and the year 2001, such as the unjust process of 'racial profiling,' or "the issue of police stopping minorities for no reason other than their race" or color, to ticket and bully or vex them. Indeed, it became so bad that the ACLU concluded that the legitimacy of the entire justice system was threatened. (Johnson, 1999, p. 3A)

Although most states said the problem was limited and didn't "warrant special legislation," the dehumanizing practice of 'racial profiling' continued throughout the beginning of the new millennium—that is, up until the beginning of the Race War of 2010. I believe white leaders in most of the United States were in denial about the problems of racism. Black people, however, in many states began to resist overwhelmingly the discriminatory practices, which created racial hostilities, and they started the underground guerrilla forces which later, and routinely, attacked police departments across the nation, picking off and politically assassinating some of the so-called 'finest men' in blue, especially those who habitually abused and used excessive force against blacks. It essentially became a killing spree.

These terrible events and activities tore apart the fabric of our fragile democracy and American society for a while. And then there was the backlash by the police that fostered ill-will toward law enforcement organizations everywhere. No one of color could trust or even believe in the various police and law enforcement agencies anymore. They became essentially a joke. And our state and federal prisons began to fill up with black men and women, and other racial groups.

The problem was exacerbated when more state and federal prisons were built in the country to house nonwhites and other minorities because of harsh sentences by various state and federal judiciaries and courts. This proved (to be) the *undoing* of our criminal justice system, as it did not deter crime in the United States whatsoever. Political economist Rodger Doyle summed it all up when he wrote:

> The most obvious result of harsh sentencing is the disruption of the black community, particularly as it bears on young black men. A substantial minority of both white and black teenage boys engage in violent behavior. In their twenties, most whites give up violence as they take on the responsibility of jobs and families, but a disproportionate number of African Americans do not have jobs, and they are most likely to contribute to crime and imprisonment rates. The system is biased against blacks in other ways, such as in sentencing for drug offenses: although 13 percent of drug users in the U.S. are black, blacks account for 74 percent of all those sentenced to prison for drug offenses.

One in seven adult black males has lost his voting rights because of a felony conviction. (1999, p. 25)

What exactly was the fairness in our criminal justice system when you had statistics like the absurd ones mentioned by Doyle in 1999? I mean what black person could have been rehabilitated with these biased and unpleasant odds? In a word, these things just upset and pissed black people off. It was certainly a part of the problem, not the needed solution. And it became a black eye on our nation.

Even more damaging was the pattern of police brutality which continued almost unabated against African Americans. I recall, as I was in junior high school then, the shooting, by white police, of Maurice Green in Chicago, the rape and torture of Abner Louima in a Brooklyn, New York, police station in 1997. Although Louima did not die, the ramming of a stick in his rectum destroyed his intestines. Remember that? The white policemen who were charged denied—at first—that the incident even occurred, claiming it might have happened when he resisted arrest, supposedly en route to the police station. But later one of the white cops admitted to the heinous crime and was sentenced to several years in prison. The white community of New York, of course, and if you can imagine, was thoroughly outraged.

Then there was the fatal shooting of a mentally ill (but college-educated) black woman. She was apparently shot by a bicycle patrol cop who confronted the tiny, homeless Margaret Mitchell over a shopping cart in 1999. (Kasindorf, 1999, p. 3A) Or perhaps you remembered the shooting of Tyisha Miller by mostly white policemen in Riverside, California, as she sat in her car at a gas station.

Furthermore, I don't think *anyone* could forget the gunning down of black West African immigrant Amadon Diallo in Bronx, New York. Diallo was unarmed, but the white, New York policemen fired over forty rounds of ammunition at him, killing him instantly. So you *did* see a pattern of accessive force on the part of many law enforcement agencies throughout the United States? Maybe blacks felt they had a score to settle with white America? But there were other incidents and hate crimes, that I remembered, Youngblood. One was the dragging death of James Byrd, Jr. in Texas by white racist John William King and two other of his white cronies. Although King and two others involved received the death penalty, it did not appease the black community of Jasper, Texas, or blacks in the nation.

Or bear in mind, for instance, the murderous rampages of WCOTC activist and white racist Benjamin Nathaniel Smith, who deliberately (and some would say diabolically) killed a black man and an Asian man and wounded nine other minorities across Illinois and Indiana in 1999. And who could forget the brutal attack of Lance Corporal Carlos Colbert, the black Marine, who was serving our country, no less, in 1999, but was left for dead by "a [crazed] group of whites armed with brass knuckles and chanting 'white power'" (Herbert, 1999, p. A19). Colbert survived, barely, as a paraplegic. If you ask me, those hoodlums were just a bunch of cowards.

Although the sporadic death of whites by the hands of callous and heartless blacks happened at intervals, nothing could quite make-up for the death of black people by law-enforcement officials, or those whites who indirectly supported such conduct. Then there was police officer Jeffrey Cooperstein, a white man, "suspected of authoring a Web page with racist overtones [who] was arrested in the shooting death of black motorist [Deron Grimmitt]" during the 1990s. (Officer held, 1999, p. 17A) Moreover, an investigative report in 1996 by the inspector general's office of the United States Justice Department discovered that white law enforcement officers (four African Americans even [sic] attended) engaged in racist, licentious and puerile behavior during that year's annual "Good O'Boys Roundup" (Justice Report, 1996, p. 7A). The late syndicated columnist Carl Rowan succinctly explained:

> Thousands of law enforcement people from members of local police forces to agents of the FBI and Bureau of Alcohol, Tobacco and Firearms (BATF) participated in [that] "good ol' country boys" roundups in the hills of Tennessee. [This] annual get-together featured T-shirts showing Dr. Martin Luther King's face behind a target and O.J. [Simpson] in a hangman's noose. "Nigger hunting licenses" were sold, along with other items that degraded African Americans. (Rowan, 1996, p. 196)

Therefore, with Justice Department Officers attending and participating in that racist event, who needed the justice system? We should have hung our heads in shame if these individuals were our finest, or the best that our criminal justice system had to offer. African American psychiatrists William H. Grier and Price M. Cobbs wrote that: "it is necessary for a black man in America to develop a profound distrust of his white fellow citizens and of the nation. He must be on guard to protect himself against physical hurt. He must cushion himself against cheating, slander, humiliation, and outright mistreatment by the official representatives of society.... Every black man in America has suffered such injury as to be realistically sad about the hurt done him. He must, however, live in spite of the hurt and so he learns to know his tormentor exceedingly well..." (Grier & Cobbs, 1968, p. 149).

I also should point out that the opening up of the Internet to racist bigots allowed for the technological proliferation of Web hate sites (Web sites, 1999, p. 12A) and an increase in the hate groups' rolls (or membership), especially those of white supremacist groups. This was probably so because whites had more wealth and ready access to more computers and the Internet. It was disturbing and alarming. And we were mistaken to think such concerns were overblown. Somehow, I think we should have closed this avenue down—period!

All in all, the fatal police shootings across the nation were not just aberrations; and absolutely unnecessary, if you ask me, but also ammunition for the numerous and detestable incidents of the late 1990s, inflaming the abhorrent racial tensions that led to the Race War of 2010. Black people, as you very well know, have long memories. Therefore, they will *never* forget these tragic events.

Youngblood, I know the way that I am recalling these events might seem sort of one-sided, but I can only give you what I think is the "black perspective," or my point of view. In any case, at that time, we were in a perpetual crisis; and as I read in an old newspaper clipping, a little known African American senator from the state of Nevada named Joe Neal predicted in 1997 that "a race war [was] coming to the United States unless whites and blacks [began] to reach out to understand each other. Neal went on to say that, if we [didn't] address the [racial] problem in a few years we will undergo one of the most devastating tragic incidents, a race war" (Vogel, 1997, p. 2A).

These prophetic words by Senator Neal were quoted in an article by journalist Ed Vogel back in 1997, and he was absolutely right. White supremacists, of course, had no problem with the idea or notion of a race war, as they thought whites were God's chosen people, and that all other races of people were lowly beasts, mud-people, sub-human, and deserving elimination. They also believed that a holy race war was inevitable, as they wanted to cleanse and save the world. How ridiculous. But I suppose racists all over the world have wanted to eradicate blacks or other so-called beastly races. I personally believe, however, that this will *never* happen because when one race is completely destroyed, or totally exterminated, so will the entire human race. Or this is what I believed.

Although some states seriously instituted hate crime laws, they were done haphazardly, or reluctantly and halfheartedly, but mostly, such needed laws were hard to implement and enforce. Later, of course, we found out that this was a terrible mistake. And to make matters worse, black and white people *never* saw things the same way, or eye-to-eye. One example I know you might remember is the infamous O.J. Simpson trials, where "blacks rejoiced after the first trial in which Simpson was found innocent of criminal charges...while whites rejoiced over [the] verdict against him in the civil trial" (Vogel, 1997, p. 2A). Inexplicably, according to journalist Robert Scheer back in 1996, "the main gap between whites and blacks [in America was] one of perception. While most blacks [asserted] that racism [remained] an impediment to progress, whites overwhelmingly [thought] that view [was] rubbish" (Scheer, 1996, p. 28). Ironically, whites in many states felt like beleaguered minorities though they controlled everything and outnumbered blacks and other minorities.

In many critical ways, these controversial things showed the enormous racial split that began to develop in America. Some white Americans, for the most part, believed that economic and social parity had been achieved among the races in the 1990s, but according to an important study by labor economist Jared Bernstein of the nonpartisan Economic Policy Institute in 1995, black citizens still trailed "whites in wages and employment opportunities...despite significantly closing the educational gap" (U.S. Report Says, 1995). Berstein overwhelmingly attributed this disparity to "job discrimination and labor market trends that more adversely affect[ed] blacks" (U.S. Reports Says, 1995).

Even more important, perhaps whites during this time thought that Affirmative Action was "a threat to their job security in a [supposedly] shrinking economy. But for blacks, affirmative action [had] been a ladder up out of poverty, and most [didn't] want it withdrawn" (Scheer, 1995) during those hapless times. These facts didn't matter to right-wing extremists and many hot-blooded Anglo Saxon Whites in America and some conservative Blacks. However, these things did not go unnoticed by angry black people. Nor did a study, sponsored by the embattled NAACP and conducted by Hamilton College in New York and the polling firm of Zogby International. According to the 1999 study, "50 percent of whites surveyed responded that general separation by race [was] acceptable, compared with about 40 percent of blacks" (Half Young Adults, 1999, p. 3A). But could anyone believe in such contentious figures? Apparently people *did* believe.

I cannot fathom the attitudes and how, after the many racial gains in the United States, young adults, of all races, believed that segregation of the races was "acceptable as long as there [were] equal opportunities for everyone" (Half Young Adults, 1999, p. 3A)? "What were these young people thinking?" I wondered. Somehow, I wanted to force everyone of them, at least those who participated in the Hamilton College survey, to read and study the Plessy vs. Ferguson case, where the U.S. Supreme Court condoned or sanctioned inequality and racial separatism. As we found out, it was the wrong thing to do. Those were not pleasant times, Youngblood, and I dare say we, as a nation, wanted to return to them, because ultimately (and usually) black people got the short end of the stick. That is to say, things were not equal for African Americans, who had no serious part in the political process of the nation at that time. How could we have assured equal opportunity anyway?

In either case, the acceptance of racial separatism was eventually and energetically embraced by almost everyone in the year 2008, as supposedly the only right and feasible means of solving the race problem in America. In the end, it became harmful to race relations and harmful to our society. I guess white political scientist Andrew Hacker was right when he wrote back in 1992 that:

> Black Americans are Americans, yet they still subsist as aliens in the only land they know. Other groups may remain outside the mainstream—some religious sects, for example—but they do so voluntarily. In contrast, blacks must endure a segregation that is far from freely chosen. So America may be seen as two separate nations. Of course, there are places where the races mingle. Yet in most significant respects, the separation is pervasive and penetrating. As a social and human division, it surpasses all others—even gender—in intensity and subordination. (Hacker, 1992, p. 3)

The gravity or full weight of these terrible contradictions, incidents, and events built up and marked the beginning of the American Race War of 2010. It didn't matter that some "white supremacists accused of plotting to set up a whites-only Republic in the Pacific Northwest" were arrested, found guilty and thrown in Jail (White Supremacists Guilty, 1999, p. 12A); or that members of the Ku Klux Klan lost much of their property in Alabama and other places for the lynching of blacks, or that many white racists were given substantial jail time for satanic cross-burnings, or that rogue white racists committed suicide after some committed mass murders. The situation slowly became uncontrollable, or untenable. However, those who died fighting became famous martyrs in the white supremacist movement.

Though not obvious at the time, Attorney Morris Dees, one of the founders of the Southern Poverty Law Center, did his part in trying to turn the tides of a Modern-day Holocaust by going after and prosecuting the guilty parties on both sides. I was just reading the other day a clipping from *USA Today*, dated February 15, 1999, about how Dees crippled the Aryan Nations of North Idaho on behalf of Victoria Kennan and her son Jason, as they were scared out of their wits and ruthlessly terrorized by the undaunted and criminal members of the Aryan Nation. (McMahon, 1999, p. 4A) Many others also became targets of terror. Therefore, what Dees tried to do was commendable, but it was not enough. Maybe we should have started more hate-fighting interest groups like the NAACP and the indelible Southern Poverty Law Center.

Youngblood, I must also admit that before the 'times of war,' and long before Morris Dees' good works, several inspired novelists like Lloyd Zimpel in his 1973 book, *Meeting the Bear: Journal of the Black Wars*, or Sam Greenlee's 1969 novel, *The Spook Who Sat By The Door*, and even avowed white racist and intrepid author Andrew MacDonald—or former physics professor William Pierce's—unsophisticated novel, *The Turner Diaries*, envisioned the impending dangers of racial strife in the United States. *The Turner Diaries'* speculative imaginings, of course, became the 'manifesto' for white racists everywhere, especially those who wanted to start a racial war in America. The FBI even found a copy of the book in the possession of Timothy McVeigh, the famous mass-murderer, who heartlessly bombed the Oklahoma City Federal building, as the book, I know, was used as a blueprint for the death and destruction McVeigh inflicted. When McVeigh was finally executed by lethal injection, he, too, was declared a martyr for the 'white patriotic' cause and movement by white racist groups. Offering a way to use *The Turner Diaries* as a teaching tool or vehicle to prevent a race war in America, the famous black journalist Carl T. Rowan wrote in 1996 that:

> If we Americans [were] ever to escape the threat of "Armageddon" and "the rivers of blood" that *The Turner Diaries* predicted, we [must have] early and massive interventions in the lives of the millions of children who constitute a hopeless underclass. [I]nterventions [should take place] at home, in schools, and in teenage life choices. [Furthermore], the education and lifestyle initiatives [should] be financed in part by government, in part by private institutions, and otherwise carried out by volunteers. (Rowan, 1996, pp. 291-292)

The bold interventions suggested by Rowan, however, never took place, much to my considerable chagrin. In fact, his classic 1996 book, *The Coming Race War in America* was thought of by many as the ravings of a paranoid old black man with a delusional mind, despite rave reviews and praise for the book. Nonetheless, the late Rowan's dire prognosis was right all along—that is, "the United States [was] hopelessly doomed to implode in an Armageddon of racial strife" (Rowan, 1996, p. 244). The late black novelist James Baldwin predicted (some say he caused) the L.A. or Watts Riots of 1965 in his important and revolutionary book of 1963, *The Fire Next Time*, but no one was paying attention or listening then either. And because of such apathy, the place gradually imploded in racial violence. It became the "Fire Right Now."

The late white racist William Pierce (or Andrew MacDonald) fancifully concluded in his bitter, hate-filled and disturbing book, *The Turner Diaries*, that black guerrilla fighters, in retaliation for the murder of black leaders, would start the race war in America. And he was right on that particular score, especially when "a rash of white-supremacist assassinations of prominent black leaders" actually took place. (Rowan, 1996, p. 283) Some of the first to be summarily put to death, lynched, for no other reason than being the wrong skin color, were the many black conservatives, even as they loudly protested and supported the anti-government rhetoric, which was steeped in the racism of cursed White Supremacy. Next came the black liberal intellectuals and Muslim population. Finally, several prominent Jews were lined up and shot for good measure.

However, what Pierce and other white racists didn't envision or count on was the intervention and brilliant military mechanizations and tactics of General Freeman Beckwith, and the fact that the so-called "Order," or White National Alliance would also be defeated. Indeed, what Pierce abjectly wrote and predicted in his fascist novel *The Turner Diaries* was an ideological and literary rip-off of both Lloyd Zimpel's *Meeting the Bear: Journal of The Black Wars*, and Greenlee's *The Spook Who Sat By The Door*. What you have in all these similar works is the same kind of Race-War scenarios, with only different outcomes. Greenlee's prophetic novel still sent chills up my spine when I re-read it recently. He eloquently sums up exactly what I have been trying to impart in this letter, Younglood. Greenlee bombastically wrote in 1969:

> Whitey was stupid and stubborn about Negroes [or Blacks]. He would not believe that Negroes would not continue to passively accept the pushing around that whites had come to think of as their birthright. The white cops...felt that all they had to do was to charge the [black] people here, make enough arrests of the ringleaders, bloody enough heads, a bit of tear gas, guns fired overhead and if need be, shoot a few niggers and they would tuck their tails between their legs and become silent and invisible once more. They would not believe that things had changed and that these people had had enough. (Greenlee, 1969 and 1990, p. 154)

The horrific vision of the future was further expressed by the prophet of doom writer, Lloyd Zimpel, when he wrote about "What Black People Must Do." He suggested that when the American Race War and devastation began:

Every Black Man in the Resistance [should be] prepared to lay his life on the line for Black Freedom from racist violence perpetrated by whites. Every Black resident…must organize to support the brave Freedom Fighters who will face the machine guns, tanks, flame throwers, napalm and grenades of the mad pig cops and soldiers. (Zimpel, 1971 and 1973, pp. 131-132)

Zimpel also talked about the possibility of biological or germ warfare in a racial war, such as the strategic use of botulism, which would systematically kill people. And this cataclysmic concept or nightmarish means of waging war also became all too real when the white racist group, Fourth of July Militia Brigade released the infectious Anthrax disease into the atmosphere in Michigan in 2004, and killed over half of the black population of Detroit, Michigan. Many unvaccinated whites died, too. I wonder if the Fourth of July Militia Brigade understood that they could have wiped-out the entire U.S. population with the deadly Anthrax? Sadly, the United States government did not have enough anthrax vaccine to inoculate all American citizens. Perhaps we should have tried to rid ourselves of racial ignorance or abandon our prejudices to understand what Hacker was trying to impart in 1992 when he wrote:

America is inherently a "white" country: in character, in structure, in culture. Needless to say, black Americans create lives of their own. Yet, as a people, they face[d] boundaries and constrictions set by the white majority…. That racial tensions cast a pall upon this country [could] hardly be denied. People…vent feeling of hostility and anger that in the past they repressed. (Hacker, 1992, p. 4)

Perhaps we underestimated the problem. Or maybe as I mentioned earlier, 'complacency' became our real enemy. As it happened, Americans did not have the will or inclination to stop the advent of the Race War of 2010. What transpired prior to this catastrophic event certainly revealed the ugliness of American Race Relations. It was certainly a reflection of the deterioration of American racial harmony. Black scholar and folklorist Julius Lester wrote back in 1968 that:

The race war, if it comes will come partly from the necessity for revenge. You can't do what has been done to blacks and not expect retribution. The very act of retribution is liberating, and perhaps it is no accident that the symbolism of Christianity speaks of being washed in Blood as an act of purification. Psychologically, blacks have always found an outlet for their revenge whenever planes have fallen, autos have collided, or just every day when white folks die. (Lester, 1968, p. 137)

Inevitably, it became so bad in almost every major city that the American people took to the streets, with their various grudges, and large caches of deadly military-type weapons and explosives, gunning down anyone who looked different. Snipers were everywhere, taking random and deadly shots at people, and bloody street-fighting battles and motor attacks took place. I guess it was similar to war-torn Bosnia during the late 1990s—everywhere, night and day. Essentially, it became the order and business of the hour and day. It seemed everything spiraled out of control, as atrocities of unimaginable proportion were committed. It became America's worst nightmare. What went wrong? A lot of things, I suppose. I read somewhere that a Chinese philosopher (or sage) once said that with every crisis comes a great opportunity, but I didn't see the logic in those words until much later. And because of the chaos that went on in the United States, General Freeman Beckwith stepped in to the deadly fray to stop the craziness, the madness, and save what he thought would be *all* black people in America—to stop, what he called: The Black Holocaust. In essence, it became an opportunity. Columnist Ray Willis, in 1997, wrote:

> There is no mistaking that the Black Holocaust [was] one of the most under-reported tragedies in the history of the world.... That's why...more than ever before, our story should be told—unfiltered, unedited, unexpurgated. The Jews have done an admirable job of making the world remember their Holocaust. Black people most also learn never to forget. (1997, p. 11)

For the sake of clarity, let me talk a bit about the infamous General Beckwith. It seems like only yesterday that I was working as General Beckwith's aide at the Pentagon—the cursed Puzzle-Palace as it is sometimes called—and I knew his intimate thoughts more than anyone. I also should have known that my career as an Army officer was over as soon as I joined forces with General Beckwith's troops to form a new black state. I admit I didn't know everything. But I remember when the idea of creating a sovereign government or black nation first germinated in Beckwith's mind. I recall him saying, "We will be the catalyst of change for the betterment of blacks everywhere in the world." I also remember him mentioning an article that he had clipped from *The Chronicle of Higher Education*, dated January 26, 1996.

There was a particular passage that almost drove Beckwith insane, as he thought of himself as a devout Christian, and it angered him (to no end) if you ask me to think that white racists believed they were Christians. Wasn't this an oxymoron, or joke in fact? Or for racists, it was a contradiction in terms. Jewish professor and research scientist Raphael S. Ezekiel pointed out in that article, entitled, "Talking About Race With America's Klansmen," that many whites mistakingly believed in Christian Identity, which supposedly "provides divine endorsement for white supremacy: Racist behavior [they also insist] is Christian love, since as one of the Klan calling cards announces, "God is a racist" (Ezekeil, 1996, p. B3).

"What stupidity," the General would rant and rave. Indeed, how could people hate solely because of a person's skin color? And base it on the teachings of Christ? Beckwith would ask. The racist message of the Christian Identity movement and philosophy left him completely rattled. Especially because Christ was not a racist, and he *was* Jewish. Yes, Youngblood, I understood Beckwith's feelings and indignation that such racist ideology was being embraced and attributed to Christ. I mean, Youngblood, it doesn't make sense from any humane standpoint. Besides, Christianity does not teach violence and murder, or religious hatred. Nor did Christ condone or teach such discriminatory rubbish. General Beckwith came to believe that in life and dealing with racist types, you must go straight for their jugular to get them off your neck.

As the second black man to become chairman of the Joint Chiefs of Staff, General Beckwith had triumphed over adversity and those who had tried to defeat him, break his spirit, make him quit the military, and give up his hard-won officer commission. But Beckwith had fooled them all, beaten them by the sheer force of his will. To be sure, the old white boy's network had all tried to stop him in his tracks, but their obsequious gamble had failed because of a President who had implicitly trusted and believed in him and given him the coveted job as the military chairman. (What, Beckwith told me, would President Henry Futler think when he learned of his New African Republic?)

General Beckwith had an overriding reason to succeed as an officer, a fervent belief in the importance of doing well in every endeavor he undertook, and a particular disdain for those who relied on handouts. Nevertheless, Beckwith had a big heart and, above all, he had compassion, even as he amassed political power. He was a political animal.

The General was a tall black man with curly black hair that grayed at his temples. At fifty-one years of age he was a definite presence, and the youngest Chairman of the Joint Chiefs of Staff—ever! His rise to power had been meteoric, and unlike any other officer's rise to prominence, with the possible exception of perhaps Generals MacArthur, Marshall, Eisenhower, or Powell. In a nutshell, Beckwith became a *cause celebre* after his anticipated appointment.

However, living the life of the top military man in 2008, at Quarters six at Fort Myers, Virginia, the residence of every Chairman of the Joint Chiefs of Staff, was a sham to him. That is to say, Beckwith knew he could not go on living a lie. Indeed, it was hypocritical and went against everything he stood for, what he truly believed, and represented. His lesser black brethren and those fighting oppression deserved just as much. It was tearing him up inside. But Beckwith had understood what he was going to do all along.

And Beckwith's credibility on Capitol Hill—despite the racist and murderous events going on around him—was the best since the nation had had a fascination with General Powell, the first Black Chairman of the Joint Chiefs of Staff, hero of the Gulf War, and former Secretary of State. Beckwith also became a part of the President's inner circle. Other black officers had been mesmerized by General Beckwith's summons, his call to arms, and they too had been convinced that a racial war was imminent. General Beckwith proclaimed that a black nation was the only way blacks in America would ever survive. We had all become co-opted, bamboozled. I think political columnist Tom Wicker explained it best when he wrote back in 1996 that:

> Given the history of Negroes [blacks] in America, younger blacks naturally were eager to be free of conditions that had limited their forebears' lives. So they banded together (with an American faith in organization) in the various forms of the black power movement.

It was also natural that given the same history, whites resented and feared black power rhetoric…. In fact, the [new] black power movement was a direct, not merely implicit, challenge to what Kenneth Clark cited as the prerequisite of the of stable black-white relationship: tacitly acknowledged white superiority, tacitly accepted black inferiority. Few whites had imagined *that* bedrock could crumble, even after desegregation in faraway Dixieland. (Wicker, 1996, p. 90)

The general had also learned that once you commit yourself in doing something then you do it and do not pussyfoot around. So in trying to establish a black nation, and seceding from the United States, Beckwith followed a carefully scripted plan, rooted in the lessons he had learned from his dangerous experiences in the Gulf War: It required decisive action, as well as the pretense of warding-off an evasion from Cuba; and once started, there would be no turning back.

General Beckwith talked without equivocation about the need for the build-up in the Southern States, because of the so-called growing threat from Cuba. Such a build up was not kindly looked upon by most Americans. Giving the Congress his professional estimate of the situation, Beckwith left out the fact that he had established several secret military installations for his black armies in the South. As the Chairman of the Joint Chiefs of Staff, Beckwith also authorized the use of several million dollars of discretionary funds for the transfer of troops to Louisiana, Tennessee, Mississippi, Alabama and Georgia. He knew that in order to succeed, he would have to work fast to accomplish what was unheard of until then—to establish a new black nation, while confronting the brutalities of American society forthrightly.

And unbeknownst to many, the General's armies had the most modern of military weapons, such as heat-seeking missiles, air-to-ground ballistic missiles that could avoid enemy radar and deliver the same destructive punch as bombers—or smart bombs—that could hunt and kill moving military targets and tanks approximately 300 miles away, with no external guidance.

The events and activities that would eventually lead up to the Race War of 2010 preoccupied General Beckwith's time, consumed his very soul. He knew he was considered by many blacks to be the white man's lackey, forgetting the black agenda. But that all changed with his plan to establish the new black nation. And as General Beckwith expected, the federal government's intelligence community failed to anticipate his actions and the impending crises.

Beckwith suddenly didn't care about the so-called great opportunities of the armed forces, supposedly provided to blacks, because they were slowly being eaten away anyway by Congressional decree. In other words, the U.S. military in less than two years, because of the ending of the draft in 2001, would be once again a hollow Army, similar to the ones after the Vietnam War, and the ending of the Cold War.

Yes, Youngblood. The armed forces were broken, irreparably ruined, and the United States was vulnerable, perhaps, to the new Chinese Superpower. In fact, a breakup of the United States and the formation of a Black State would have some very tragic consequences—like the indomitable Russia would, perhaps, be knocking on our border doors, maybe even ready to attack a country preoccupied with a Race War at home. Although the military was once considered America's showcase of multiracial, cross-class, gender, and cultural opportunities, as an institution it still believed in the Old Boys' Network, and was inherently and covertly racist. Or that is what I believed.

You might recall the President's 2010 State of the Union address a while back, where he sternly stated that even though this was an unfortunate and dangerous period in our history, the U.S. would survive. Fuller went on to warn that if the government did not prevail, the country would never be the same again, and our democratic system would fail. The President vowed to end the Race War that had started earlier in 2010, and prevent General Beckwith from dividing the nation. President Fuller finally stated that blacks "enjoyed freedom in the United States that was unparalleled anywhere else in the world, so why are they doing this? Why must they fight us?"

Upon hearing President Fuller ask *why* blacks would fight us, I could only think of what African American novelist Greenlee wrote in *The Spook Who Sat By The Door*, "Because it's war, whitey" (Greenlee, 1969 and 1990, p. 226). But I would also add: "To survive, baby!" I must also point out that only for the second time in United States' history was Martial Law declared nationally by a fearful President because of the black military rebellion and Race War of 2010. . . . I guess the president struggled with what to do about General Beckwith.

As I finish writing this letter, I am told that General Beckwith has finally been captured and incarcerated. Now I guess he will die like me. His black armies, I am told, have scattered, fleeing the southern states they once occupied. Some have even left the country. The media has reported that a vast quantity of sophisticated weaponry (a formidable arsenal) which contributed to the initial success of General Beckwith's armies was also confiscated. In the end, the black secessionist rebels were brutally and successfully put down along with the many white supremacist factions. How could they have won anyway?

To say the least, Youngblood, I am sad. Yes, I guess I have hit rock bottom. I mean General Beckwith showed the world what he could become, an incredible piece of work, a black leader forged from the hatred and foolishness of a society that didn't seem to care about all its people—a society that lived off the fear of others. It is interesting to note that "by indulging our fears in the face of the best evidence, we live not just in a hive of disinformation but in a vast horror film in which we can shiver with the thrill of terror, secure in the knowledge that whatever is out there will not really affect us" (Gabler, 1999, p. 11B). But the Race War of 2010 did affect us all.

Moreover, our ignorance, mistreatment of blacks by whites, as well as misjudgment and apathy on all of our parts, perhaps, caused the terrible Race War of 2010. General Beckwith had been in a position to finally do something about the hatred, racism and discrimination that had plagued his life—all our lives—but it is obvious that he has failed by his recent capture. The United States government has won again, without dropping a deadly nuclear device. So in that sense, we are extremely fortunate. Perhaps the war between the races has finally come to a critical juncture, or is this all in my imagination?

Let's face it, Youngblood, racial discrimination is still so entrenched at all levels of our society that it will *never* be overcome in our life time, or maybe as long as humans exist. And I really understand that. But I'm hopeful. Youngblood, although we (Blacks) lost the battle, with over two million blacks and one million whites dying in the process of the race war, and although they have court martialed me—that is, the Army tried me for treason (being a former military officer and all), don't feel sorry for me. Black people have always fought the good fight, the fight for their place in the political, social, intellectual and economic sun in this cursed world. And I guess it will always be that way. What *else* can we possibly do?

I have decided that I won't worry about anything anymore—that is, as long as I still live. As I look back on things, I think this Race War of 2010 could have been prevented, avoided entirely. And before I conclude this letter, I want to tell you what I think we could or should have done. Perhaps we did not have the social will to institute such drastic measures and changes. First, we should have kept the *dialogue* going about race in America, no matter how much we hated it, and found a way to replace prejudice and bigotry with understanding and tolerance. Second, we should have prohibited—no, condemned, and prosecuted *any* group that committed acts of violence, or expressed racist views. Forget about the Freedom of Speech for racists. Third, our government should have made it a federal crime to communicate racial hatred over the Internet, ardently or seriously going after the leaders to bankrupt them at every possible turn, (as well as block access to such sites), and despite their First Amendment Rights. This should have included banning or curbing anti-government militia groups and their symbols of racism and extremist hatred. And ultimately, we should have eliminated discrimination, the real problem.

Furthermore, law enforcement agencies across America should have ceased and desisted racist and unfair 'racial profiling' of black Americans, despite their argument to the contrary, to reestablish the trust that is vitally needed for any effective police force. According to Grier and Cobbs, the black man in America "can never quite respect laws which have no respect for him, and laws designed to protect white men are viewed as white men's laws. To break another man's law may be inconvenient if one is caught and punished, but it can never have the moral consequences involved in breaking one's own law. (Grier & Cobbs, 1968, p. 149) White Americans, unfortunately, never understood this logic.

Perhaps more to the point, we should have deported white and black racists; or forced them to leave the country. Equally important, we should have opened up every avenue or opportunity for American citizens to grow and empower themselves through knowledge and free education. Yes, the United States government should have banned *all* racist hate literature and *any* manuscripts that might have incited groups to murder, commit violence and riot. In addition, racists should have been viewed with our suspicion and contempt! We should have also truly educated our young people about the significant contribution all ethnic or racial groups have made to this society, while working wholeheartedly for a color-blind nation.

Furthermore, we should have had many public discussions and debates about our demagogic politicians who preached intolerance of immigrants and other minority groups. They should have been criticized and censured. Indeed, they should have been held personally responsible for riling up hate crowds. Additionally, if convicted, Gun Manufacturers should have been severely fined for selling weapons of mass-destruction in poor neighborhoods. More importantly, we should have continued to protest for equality, no matter the adverse circumstances. Finally, we should have recognized, not trivialized, black rage, and not ignored the need to proclaim severe hatred by whites toward blacks as a mental health problem. Indeed, steps to treat these individuals should have been taken. As African American psychiatrists William H Grier and Price Cobbs aptly wrote (1968, p. 151):

> Contempt and hatred of black people is so thoroughly a part of the American personality that a profound convulsion of society may be required to help a dark child over his fear of the dark.

While I have been locked-up, I had the chance to read Levar Burton's (of *Star Trek: The Next Generations'* fame) interesting 1997 novel of the future, entitled *Aftermath*, and I am awed and amazed at the parallels of what really happened during the Race War and what actually took place in his fictional account. Burton, however, puts the time frame of a Race War taking place in the year 2015, after a first and imagined African American president-elect is assassinated. I am also reminded of General Beckwith when I read the following passage from Burton's brilliant novel:

> In a last-ditch effort to prevent a possible race war, General Wyatt Dixon, one of America's most distinguished black officers, attempts to seize control of

the army. His efforts fail and the United States military splits in half, with minority soldiers lining up behind Dixon. Fighting breaks out on military bases around the country. For the first time since the Civil War, American soldiers are fighting one another. (Burton, 1997, p. xi)

Sounds familiar, huh? Incredibly, even back in 1997, actor and writer Levar Burton almost had it right. But in the end, the federal government prevailed. I don't know, Youngblood, maybe our democracy is worthy of saving. In the final analysis, as Virginia's Chief Judge of the United States Fourth Circuit Court of Appeals, J. Harvie Wilkinson, once wrote:

Our early history demonstrates an important truth: that union and disunion are not two stark conditions but rather opposite ends of a continuum of national health, measured by the degree to which a nation's people place the national welfare above that of some other interest—sectional, racial, or otherwise. (Wilkinson, 1997, p. 199)

I suppose things will be different in America from now on, Youngblood. Maybe we can rebuild our society into the multicultural nation we really deserve. If only we had done all of the things that I have suggested. Perhaps we (and General Beckwith for that matter) wouldn't be in the predicament we find ourselves in today. Who knows exactly? I wish I could be there for the rebuilding. I suppose Lester was right when he wrote that "American as it exists must be destroyed. There is no other way. It is impossible to live within this country and not become a...murderer" (Lester, 1968, p. 137).

Well, I guess it's too late for me as I sit on death row. There will be no pardon or imminent reprieve. I just hope you get this letter. I hope we can overcome one day.

Yours always in the struggle,
Uncle Maximus Shakesphere

REFERENCES

Adams, Pam. "Mass Killings Make White Men Suspect," *Las Vegas Review Journal* (Thursday, August 26, 1999), p. 9B.

Baldwin, James. *The Fire Next Time*. New York: Laurel, 1963.

Burton, Lavar. *Aftermath*. New York: Warner Books, Inc., 1997.

Doyle, Rodger. "Behind Bars in the U.S. and Europe," *Scientific American* (August 1999), p. 25.

Ezekiel, Raphael S. "Talking About Race With America's Klansmen," *The Chronicle of Higher Education* (January 26, 1996), p. B3.

"FBI reaches out to militia groups in response to Oklahoma City bombing," *Las Vegas Review Journal* (Monday, July 12, 1999), p. 5A.

"Former football player Rozier says he's sorry for slayings," *Las Vegas Review Journal* (Sunday, March 7, 1999), p. 16B.

"Former NFL Player Charged in Killing," *Las Vegas Review Journal* (Wednesday, March 24, 1999), p. 10A.

Fritz, Mark. "Hate Laws Fall Victim to Lack of Enforcement," *Los Angeles Times* (Monday, August 23, 1999), p. A1 & A6.

Freenlee, Sam. *The Spook Who Sat By The Door*. Originally published in 1969 by Richard Baron Books. Published in 1990 by Wayne State University Press, Detroit, Michigan.

Gabler, Neal. "Many people have a stake in creating, sustaining fear," *Las Vegas Review Journal* (Wednesday, August 18, 1999), p. 11B.

Grier, William H. & Cobbs, Price M. *Black Rage*. New York: Bantam Book, 1968.

Hacker, Andrew. *Two Nations: Black and White, Separate, Hostile, Unequal*. New York: Charles Scribner's Sons, 1992.

"Half young adults back separatism," *Las Vegas Review Journal* (Tuesday, August 17, 1999), p. 3A.

Herbert, Bob. "Staring at Hatred," *The New York Times* (February 28, 1999), p. A19.

"Idaho white supremacists buoyed by rich racists," *Las Vegas Review Journal* (Monday, December 21, 1998), p. 5B.

Johnson, Kevin. "ACLU: Racial profiling threatens justice system," *USA Today* (Wednesday, June 2, 1999), p. 3A.

"Justice report raps 'Good Ol Boys' party," *Las Vegas Review Journal* (Thursday, March 14, 1996), p. 7A.

Kasindorf, Martin. "Fatal shooting of homeless woman sparks outrage," *USA Today* (Thursday, May 27, 1999), p. 34.

Lester, Julius. *Look Out Whitey! Black Power's Gon' Get Your Mama!* New York: The Dial Press, Inc, 1968.

Levin, Brian. "Some hatemongers Don Glossy Veneers," *USA Today* (Thursday, August 5, 1999), p. 15A.

McMahon, Patrick. "Assault, terror cited in suit against Aryan Nation," *USA Today* (Monday, February 15, 1999), p. 4A.

"Neo-Nazies to demonstrate in Washington," *Las Vegas Review Journal* (Saturday, August 7, 1999), p. 8A.

"Officer held in shooting: Black man's death probed," *Las Vegas Review Journal* (Saturday, February13, 1999), p. 17A.

Page, Clarence. "Rampage by racist had plenty of support," *Las Vegas Sun* (Sunday, July 11, 1999), p. 3D. "Not all racists have mental illness," *Las Vegas Sun* (Sunday, September 5, 1999), p. 2E.

Poussaint, Alvin F. "They Hate. They Kill. Are They Insane?" *The New York Times* (Thursday, August 26, 1999), p. A21.

Rowan, Carl T. *The Coming Race War in America*. New York: Little, Brown and Company, 1996.

Scheer, Robert. "Integration: The Big Lie," *Playboy*, Vol. 43, No. 2 (February 1996), p. 28.

Smith, John L. "Keep an eye on KKK, er, Council of Conservative Citizens," *Las Vegas Review Journal* (Tuesday, January 26, 1999), p. 1B.

Smith, Vern E & Boven, Sarah Van. "The Itinerant Incendiary: How Khallid Muhammad tried to roil New York," *Newsweek* (September 14, 1998), p. 32.

Thomas, Jo. "New Face of Terror Crimes: 'Lone Wolf' Weanedon Hate," *New York Times* (Monday, August 16, 1999), p. 1 & A16.

"U.S. report says that blacks still trail whites in job areas," *Japan Times* (Monday, May 1, 1995.

Vogel, Ed. "Neal: Race war could be nearing," *Las Vegas Review Journal* (Thursday, February 6, 1997), p. 2A.

"White supremacists guilty of murder," *Las Vegas Review Journal* (Wednesday, May 5, 1999), p. 12A.

Wicker, Tom. *Tragic Failure: Racial Integration in America*. New York: William Morrow and Company, Inc., 1996.

Wilkinson, J. Harvie, III. *One Nation Indivisible: How Ethnic Separatism Threatens America*. Reading, Massachusetts: Addison-Wesley Publishing Company, Inc., 1997.

Willis, Ray. "The Black Holocaust," *The Las Vegas Sentinel Voice* (April 10, 1997), p. 11.

Zimpel, Lloyd. *Meeting the Bear: Journal of the Black Wars*. New York: Pocket Books, 1971; and originally published by The MacMillan Company, 1973.

Bibliography

Adams, Pam. 1999, August 26. "Mass Killings Make White Men Suspect." *Las Vegas Review Journal.*

Alexander, Louis. 1975. *Beyond The Facts: A Guide to the Art of Feature Writing.* Houston, Texas: Gulf Publishing Company.

Asante, Molefi K. 1988. *Afrocentricity.* Trenton, New Jersey: Africa World Press, Inc.

Avittey, George B.N. 1992. *Africa Betrayed.* New York: St. Martin's Press.

Baker, Tamara. 1999, July 7. "There never were any 'Black Confederate Soldiers.'" *USA Today.*

Baldauf, Scott. 1999, March 9. "J.C. Watts, Jr.: For Republicans, A Different Leader." *The Christian Science Monitor.*

Baldwin, James. 1955 and 1983. *Notes of a Native Son.* Boston, Massachusetts: Beacon Press.

Baldwin, James. 1963. *The Fire Next Time.* New York: Laurel.

Barker, Lucius J., Mack H. & Tate, Katherine. 1999. *African Americans and the American Political System.* 4th edition. New Jersey: Prentice Hall, Inc.

Barzun, Jacques & Graff, Henry F. 1992. *The Modern Researcher.* 5th edition. Orlando, Florida: Harcourt Brace Jovanovich.

Bell, Derrick. 1992. *Faces at the Bottom of the Well: The Permanence of Racism.* New York: Basic Books.

Bennett, W. J. 1988. *American Education: Making It Work: A Report to the President and the American People.* Washington, D.C.: U.S. Department of Education.

Berkman, Robert I. 1987. *Find It Fast: How to Uncover Expert Information on Any Subject.* New York: Harper & Row.

Berne, Eric. 1964. *Games People Play: The Psychology of Human Relationships.* New York: Grove Press, Inc.

Berry, Mary F. & Blassingame, John W. 1982. *Long Memory: The Black Experience in America.* New York: Oxford University Press.

Bond, Julian. 1990. Where We've Been, Where We're Going: A Vision of Racial Justice in the 1990's." *Harvard Civil Rights–Civil Liberties Law Review.* Vol. 25.

Boynton, Robert S. 1995, March. "The New Intellectuals." *The Atlantic Monthly*.

Bradley, Michael. 1978. *The Iceman Inheritance: Prehistoric Sources of Western Man's Racism, Sexism and Aggression*. New York: Warner Books, Inc.

Brian, Denis. 1994. *Fair Game: What Biographers Don't Tell You*. Amherst, New York: Prometheus Books.

Brimmer, Andrew. 1985, November. "The Future of Blacks in the Public Sector." *Black Enterprise*.

Brown, Cecil. 1969. *The Life and Loves of Mr. Jiveass Nigger*. New York: Fawcett Crest Book.

Brown, Tony. 1995. *Black Lies, White Lies: The Truth According to Tony Brown*. New York: William Morrow and Company, Inc.

Budiansky, Stephen. 1993, February 1. "Pioneering Integration: When the Army Took the Lead." *U.S. News and World Report*.

Burns, James M., *et. al.* 1995. *Government By the People*. National Version, 16th edition. Englewood Cliffs, New Jersey: Prentice Hall.

Burton, Lavar. 1997. *Aftermath*. New York: Warner Books, Inc.

Ceaser, James W. 1990. *Liberal Democracy and Political Science*. Baltimore, Maryland: Johns Hopkins University Press.

Cloud, Henry. 1992. *Changes that Heal: How to Understand Your Past to Ensure a Healthier Future*. New York: Harper Paperbacks.

"College Course on Slaves Irks Blacks." 1998, November 16. *Las Vegas Review Journal*.

Coughlin, Ellen K. 1996, February 16. "Not Out of Africa." *The Chronicle of Higher Education*.

Doyle, Rodger. 1999, August. "Behind Bars in the U.S. and Europe." *Scientific American*.

"Dr. Seuss Drawings Depict Fight Against Fascism." 1999, August 16. *The Wall Street Journal*.

Early, Gerald. 1991. Introduction: *The Life and Loves of Mr. Jiveass Nigger* by Cecil Brown. New York: The Ecco Press.

Ellison, Ralph. 1987. *Going To The Territory*. New York: Vintage Books.

Ezekiel, Raphael S. 1996, January 26. "Talking About Race With America's Klansmen." *The Chronicle of Higher Education*.

"FBI reaches out to militia groups in response to Oklahoma City bombing." 1999, July 12. *Las Vegas Review Journal*.

Fischer, Claude S., Hout, Michael, Jankowski, Martin S., Lucas, Sammuel R., Swidler, Ann, & Voss, Kim. 1996. *Inequality by Design: Cracking the Bell Curve Myth*. Princeton, New Jersey: Princeton University Press.

Fisher, Roger A. 1996. *Them Damned Pictures: Explorations in American Political Cartoon Art*. North Haven, Connecticut: Archon Books.

"Former football player Rozier says he's sorry for slayings." 1999, March 7. *Las Vegas Review Journal*.

"Former NFL Player Charged in Killing." 1999, March 24. *Las Vegas Review Journal*.

Franklin, John H. & Moss, Alfred A. Jr. 1994. *From Slavery to Freedom: A History of African Americans*. 7th edition. New York: McGraw-Hill, Inc.

Fritz, Mark. 1999, August 23. "Hate Laws Fall Victim to Lack of Enforcement." *Los Angeles Times.*

Freenlee, Sam. *The Spook Who Sat By The Door.* Originally published in 1969 by Richard Baron Books. Published in 1990 by Wayne State University Press, Detroit, Michigan.

Fukuyama, Francis. 1993. *The End of History and the Last Man.* New York: Avon.

Fuller, Hoyt W. 1972. "The New Black Literature: Protest or Affirmation." *The Black Aesthetic.* Ed. Addison Gayle, Jr. New York: Anchor Books.

Fulwood, Sam III. 1995, November 10. "Frustrated Blacks Turning Away From White Society." *Las Vegas Review Journal.*

Gabler, Neal. 1999, August 18. "Many people have a stake in creating, sustaining fear." *Las Vegas Review Journal.*

Grier, William H. & Cobbs, Price M. 1968. *Black Rage.* New York: Bantam Book. Hacker, Andrew. 1995, July 10. "The Crackdown on African-Americans." *The Nation.*

Hacker, Andrew. 1992. *Two Nations: Black and White, Separate, Hostile, Unequal.* New York: Charles Scribner's sons.

"Half young adults back separatism." 1999, August 17. *Las Vegas Review Journal.*

Hare, Nathan. 1969, December. "The Challenge Of A Black Scholar." *Black Scholar.*

Harris, Eddy L. 1992. *Native Stranger: A Black American's Journey into the Heart of Africa.* New York: Simon & Schuster.

Harvey, James C. 1973. *Black Civil Rights During the Johnson Administration.* Jackson, Mississippi: University and College Press of Mississippi.

Herbert, Bob. 1999, February 28. "Staring at Hatred." *The New York Times.*

Hernton, Calvin C. 1965. *Sex and Racism in America.* New York: Grove Press, Inc.

Heywood, Andrew. 1998. *Political Ideologies: An Introduction.* New York: Worth Publishers.

Higginbotham, A. Leon, Jr. 1996. *Shades of Freedom: Racial Politics and Presumptions of the American Legal Process.* New York: Oxford University Press.

Homel, David. 1987. Introduction: *How to Make Love to A Negro* by Dany Laferriere. London: Bloomsbury Publishing, Ltd.

Howlett, Debbie. 1999, August 6. "Jackson finds new passion, new popularity." *USA Today.*

Humphreys, Christmas. 1992. *Zen: A Way Of Life.* Chicago, Illinois: NTC Publishing Group.

"Idaho white supremacists buoyed by rich racists." 1998, December 21. *Las Vegas Review Journal.*

Jackson, Kennell. 1996. *America Is Me: 170 Fresh Questions and Answers on Black American History.* New York: Harper Collins.

Johnson, Charles. 1988. *Being and Race: Black Writing Since 1970.* Indianapolis: Indiana University Press.

Johnson, Kevin. 1999, June 2. "ACLU: Racial profiling threatens justice system." *USA Today.*

Jonas, Gerald. 1973. *Visceral Learning: Toward A Science Of Self-Control.* New York: The Viking Press.

Jordan, Winthrop D. Introduction: *Black/White Sex* by Grace Halsell. Greeenwich, Connecticut: A Fawcett Crest Book.

"Justice report raps 'Good Ol Boys' party." 1996, March 14. *Las Vegas Review Journal.*

Kasindorf, Martin. 1999, May 27. "Fatal shooting of homeless woman sparks outrage." *USA Today.*

Kennedy, Randall. May, 1997. "My Race Problem—and Ours." *The Atlantic Monthly.*

King, James C. 1981. *The Biology of Race.* Revised edition. Los Angeles, California: University Press.

Kuttner, Robert. 2000. "Why Liberals Need Radicals." *The American Prospect.*

Laferriere, Dany. 1987. *How to Make Love to A Negro.* Trans. David Homel. London: Bloomsbury Publishing, Ltd.

Lang, Perry. 1991, July 6. "Black Conservatives in Spotlight." *San Francisco Chronicle.*

Lasser, William. 1996. *American Politics.* Lexington, Massachusetts: D.C. Heath and Company.

Lester, Julius. 1968. *Look Out Whitey! Black Power's Gon' Get Your Mama!* New York: The Dial Press, Inc.

Levin, Brian. 1999, August 5. "Some hatemongers Don Glossy Veneers." *USA Today.*

Lipsitz, George. 1998. *The Possessive Investment in Whiteness: How White People Profit From Identity Politics.* Philadelphia: Temple University Press.

MacGregor, Morris J. Jr. 1981. *Integration of the Armed Forces 1940–1965.* Washington, D.C.: Center of Military History, United States Army.

Marable, Manning. 1999. *Black Leadership: Four Great American Leaders and the Struggle for Civil Rights.* New York: Penguin Books.

Marable, Manning. 1999. First published, 1920. "Introduction." *W.E.B. Du Bois Darkwater: Voices From Within the Veil.* Mineola, New York: Dover Publications, Inc.

Maslow, Abraham H. 1968. *Toward a Psychology of Being.* New York: Van Nostrand Reinhold Company.

May, Rollo. 1983. *The Discovery of Being: Writings in Existential Psychology.* New York: W. W. Norton and Company.

Mayfield, Julian. 1961, April. "Challenge to Negro Leadership: The Case of Robert Williams." *Commentary.* No. 3.

Mayfield, Julian. 1972. "You Touch My Black Aesthetic and I'll Touch Yours." *The Black Aesthetic.* Ed. Addison Gayle, Jr. New York: Anchor Books.

McDonald, Kim A. 1998, October 30. "Genetically Speaking, Race Doesn't Exist." *The Chronicle of Higher Education.* p. A19.

McMahon, Patrick. 1999, February 15. "Assault, terror cited in suit against Aryan Nation." *USA Today.*

McPherson, James M. 1965. *The Negro's Civil War: How American Negroes Felt and Acted During the War for the Union.* New York: Vintage Books. Note also that McPherson points out that blacks served in the Confederacy mainly because of "local patriotism and the hope of better treatment. But there is also evidence that pressure from local [white] officials and fear of impressment played a part in the decision of some Southern [Blacks] to volunteer" (p. 24).

Montagu, Ashley. 1997. *Man's Most Dangerous Myth: The Fallacy of Race.* 6th edition. Walnut Creek, California: Alta Mira Press.

Morrison, Toni. 1995. "The Site of Memory." *Inventing the Truth: The Art and Craft of Memoir.* William Zinsser, editor. 2nd edition. New York: Houghton Mifflin Company.

Murphy, John P. 1990. *Pragmatism: From Pierce to Dardson.* Boulder, Colorado: Westview Press.

Naison, Mark D. 1996. "The Significance of the Personal for the Professional." Paul A. Cimbala and Robert F. Himmelberg, editors. *Historians and Race: Autobiography and the Writing of History.* Bloomington and Indianapolis: Indiana University Press.

"Neo-Nazies to demonstrate in Washington." 1999, August 7. *Las Vegas Review Journal.*

"Officer held in shooting: Black man's death probed." 1999, February 13. *Las Vegas Review Journal.*

Page, Clarence. 1999, July 11. "Rampage by racist had plenty of support." *Las Vegas Sun.* 1999, September 5. "Not all racists have mental illness." *Las Vegas Sun.*

Pfaff, William. 1969, October. "The Decline of Liberal Politics." *Commentary.* Vol. 48, No. 4.

Poussaint, Alvin F. 1999, August 26. "They Hate. They Kill. Are They Insane?" *The New York Times.*

Prestage, Jewell L. 1968, December. "Black Politics and the Kerner Report Concerns and Direction." *Social Science Quarterly.* Vol. 49.

Raspberry, William. 1987, February 25. "The Civil Rights Movement Is Over." *The Washington Post.*

Ravitch, Diane. 1990. "Multiculturalism: E. Pluribus Plures." *American Scholar.*

Reed, Adolph. 1995, April 11. "The Current Crisis of the Black Intellectual." *Village Voice.* 1991, January 21. "False Prophet: The Rise of Louis Farrakhan." *The Nation.*

Richburg, Keith B. 1997. *Out of America: A Black Man Confronts Africa.* New York: Basic Books.

"Role of Black Confederates Questioned." 1999, February 21. *Las Vegas Review Journal.* Rollins, Richard. editor. 1994. *Black Southerners in Gray: Essays on Afro-Americans in Confederate Armies.* Redondo Beach, California: Rank and File Publications.

Rowan, Carl T. 1996. *The Coming Race War in America.* New York: Little, Brown and Company.

Sartre, Jean-Paul. 1956. *Being and Nothingness: The Major Text of Existentialism.* Translated by Hazel E. Barnes. New York: Gramercy Books.

Scheer, Robert. 1996, February. "Integration: The Big Lie." *Playboy,* Vol. 43, No. 2.

Schwartz, Marilyn. 1995. *Guidelines for Bias-Free Writing.* Bloomington: Indiana University Press.

Sitkoff, Harvard. 1971, Nevember. "Harry Truman and the Election of 1948: The Coming of Age of Civil Rights in American Politics." *The Journal of Southern History.* Vol. 37.

Sleeper, Jim. 1997. *Leberal Racism.* New York: Viking.

Smiley, Tavis. 1996. *Hard Left: Straight Talk about the Wrongs of the Rights.* New York: Anchor Books, Doubleday.

Smith, John L. 1999, January 26. "Keep an eye on KKK, er, Council of Conservative Citizens." *Las Vegas Review Journal.*

Smith, Sande. 1994. editor. *Who's Who in African-American History.* New York: Smith-Mark Publisher, Inc.

Smith, Vern E & Boven, Sarah Van. 1998, September 14. "The Itinerant Incendiary: How Khallid Muhammad tried to roil New York." *Newsweek.*

Sowell, Thomas. 1990, October 29. "Led and Misled." *The New York Times.*

Staples, Brent. 1995, January. "This Is Not A Test." *Essence Magazine.*

Steel, Shelby. 1990, May. "Ghettoized By Black Unity." *Harper's Magazine.*

The Secret Art of Dr. Seuss. 1995. Introduction by Maurice Sendak. New York: Random House.

The Sneetches and Other Stories. 1989. Dr. Seuss, catalogued by the Library of Congress as Geisel, Theodor Seuss. New York: Random House.

Thomas, Cal. 1999, February 23. "New slave on a new government plantation." *Las Vegas Review Journal.*

Thomas, Jo. 1999, August 16. "New Face of Terror Crimes: 'Lone Wolf' Weanedon Hate." *New York Times.*

"U.S. report says that blacks still trail whites in job areas." 1995, May 1. *Japan Times.*

Vaughan, Alden T. 1995. *Roots of American Racism: Essays on the Colonial Experience.* New York: Oxford University Press.

Vogel, Ed. 1997, February 6. "Neal: Race war could be nearing." *Las Vegas Review Journal.*

Walton, Anthony. 1999, January. "Technology Versus African-Americans." *The Atlantic Monthly.* Vol. 283, No. 1.

Walzer, Michael. 1960, Summer. "The Politics of the New Negro." *Dissent.*

Weidenborner, Stephen & Caruso, Domenick. 1994. *Writing Research Papers: A Guide to the Process.* 4th edition. New York: St. Martin's Press.

West, Cornel. 1989. *The American Evasion of Philosophy: A Genealogy of Pragmatism.* Madison, Wisconsin: The University of Wisconsin Press.

West, Cornel. 1993. *Keeping Faith: Philosophy and Race in America.* New York: Routledge.

White, Jack E. 2000, May. "Was Lincoln A Racist?" *Time.*

"White supremacists guilty of murder." 1999, May 5. *Las Vegas Review Journal.*

Wicker, Tom. 1996. *Tragic Failure: Racial Integration in America.* New York: William Morrow and Company, Inc.

Wilkinson, J. Harvie, III. 1997. *One Nation Indivisible: How Ethnic Separatism Threatens America.* Reading, Massachusetts: Addison-Wesley Publishing Company, Inc.

Williams, Chancellor. 1987. *The Destruction of Black Civilization: Great Issues of A Race From 4500 B.C. To 2000 A.D.* Chicago, Illinois: Third World Press.

Willie, Charles V. 1978. "The Inclining Significance of Race." *Society.* Vol. 15, No. 3.

Willis, Ray. 1997, April 10. "The Black Holocaust." *The Las Vegas Sentinel Voice.*

Wright, Ellen & Fabre, Michel. editors. 1997. *Richard Wright Reader.* New York: DaCapo Press.

Wright, Richard. 1940 and 1965. *Uncle Tom's Children.* Back flap. New York: Harper and Row Publishers.

Zimpel, Lloyd. 1971. *Meeting the Bear: Journal of the Black Wars.* New York: Pocket Books; and originally published by The MacMillan Company, 1973.

Zinn, Howard. 1990. *The Politics of History.* 2nd edition. Urbana and Chicago: University of Illinois Press.

Index

About the Author

EARNEST N. BRACEY is a retired Army Lieutenant Colonel, with over twenty years of active military service. He was commissioned through Reserve Officer Training (Distinguished Military Graduate) at Jackson State University, where he graduated with honors (Magna Cum Laude), and received his bachelor of arts degree in political science in 1974. In addition, he received the master of Public Administration in 1979 from Golden Gate University, his Masters of Arts degree in International Affairs in 1983 from the Catholic University of America, and his doctorate of Public Administration (with emphasis in Public Policy) in 1993 from George Mason University. Dr. Bracey also earned his Ph.D. in Education from Capella University in 1999.

A recipient of numerous civilian and military awards and honors, he is also a graduate of the United States Naval War College and the Command and General Staff College at Fort Leavenworth, Kansas, and previously served as Director of Administration at the prestigious Industrial College of the Armed Forces, Washington, D.C.

Dr. Bracey is Associate Professor and Chair of the Department of Political Science and History, Hampton University. He was previously professor of Political Science at the Community College of Southern Nevada in Las Vegas, where he taught American Politics and Black American History. His work has appeared in professional journals and other publications, and he is the author of the book, *Prophetic Insights: The Higher Education and Pedagogy of African Americans*, University Press of America, 1999. He also co-authored the book, *American Politics and Culture Wars* (2001). He is also the author of the novels, *Choson* (1994), and *The Black Samurai* (1998).